Inspired Cross-Stitch

30 Patterns Plus Alphabets

GAIL BUSSI

STACKPOLE BOOKS

Guilford, Connecticut

STACKPOLE BOOKS

An imprint of Globe Pequot, the trade division of The Rowman & Littlefield Publishing Group, Inc.
4501 Forbes Blvd., Ste. 200
Lanham, MD 20706
www.rowman.com

Distributed by NATIONAL BOOK NETWORK
800-462-6420

British Library Cataloguing in Publication Information available

Library of Congress Cataloging-in-Publication Data

Names: Bussi, Gail, author.
Title: Inspired cross-stitch / Gail Bussi.
Description: First edition. | Guilford, Connecticut : Stackpole Books,
  [2021] | Summary: "The 30 cross-stitch designs in Gail Bussi's signature
  hand-lettering style will encourage mindful, relaxing stitching and are
  easy enough for beginners. Each project includes chart, finished photo,
  materials list, and full instructions"— Provided by publisher.
Identifiers: LCCN 2020057560 (print) | LCCN 2020057561 (ebook) | ISBN
  9780811739504 (paper ; alk. paper) | ISBN 9780811769440 (electronic)
Subjects: LCSH: Cross-stitch—Patterns.
Classification: LCC TT778.C76 B88 2021 (print) | LCC TT778.C76 (ebook) |
  DDC 746.44/3041—dc23
LC record available at https://lccn.loc.gov/2020057560
LC ebook record available at https://lccn.loc.gov/2020057561

♾™ The paper used in this publication meets the minimum requirements of American National Standard for Information Sciences—Permanence of Paper for Printed Library Materials, ANSI/NISO Z39.48-1992.

First Edition

This book is dedicated to all
those who believe in the gift of creativity,
the power of words, and the grace of
simple everyday joys.

CONTENTS

INTRODUCTION

Writing and doing the designs for this book has been a particular joy and privilege for me, because I love words, I love design and art—and I love to stitch! So having the opportunity to create a book that combines all three is a real blessing, and I hope it will prove the same to you.

But there is more to stitching (and words) than the obvious: creativity, as we all know, is enormously therapeutic and helps create a sense of peace and well-being, even when we are going through difficult or painful times, for whatever reason. Speaking personally, I know that my designing and stitching have been a lifeline for me over the past few years, which unfortunately had some traumatic experiences and bereavements, which ultimately led to episodes of panic, anxiety, and depression. But I found that reading or writing something positive immediately improved my mood, and if I could then create a small artwork or stitched piece centered on those words, I felt even better!

Stitching (just like painting or cooking or knitting) does not necessarily solve our problems, but it makes them less painful and intrusive in the here and now, and ultimately I believe that when we feel calmer and happier, we are able to find better solutions for whatever issues we face and can move into the future with greater grace, joy, and clarity.

(Please note I am not suggesting that stitching is a replacement for appropriate medical care or medication if necessary; if you are struggling with serious issues, please do seek the help that is available out there.)

Embroidery is more than just the simple act of using a needle to pull floss through fabric: it can be a healing, creative, and joyful outlet for expressing our true selves and our passions in life. For this reason, I have chosen to focus on positive and happy words, thoughts, and affirmations, to further enhance this mindful effect.

May you find joy and peace in creating the little projects in this book for yourselves and your loved ones! Blessings and happy stitching!

Gail B

ABOUT THIS BOOK

This book is divided into three sections—Inspire, Create, and Connect—each with a different theme and focus. There is also a final section providing alphabet charts for readers who would like to create their own stitched words/quotes.

The counted cross-stitch designs in this book are all fairly simple and can be easily achieved by a confident beginner in this form of needlework. Most of the designs are done entirely in cross-stitch, with only limited use of backstitch or other specialty stitches like French knots.

I use evenweave fabric (such as Jobelan by Wichelt) and sometimes linen, in either 28-count or 32-count; that is my personal preference, but you are free to use other fabrics (such as Aida) or different stitch counts—although do bear in mind that doing so will change the finished size of the stitched design. I also use DMC embroidery floss almost exclusively; I like both the quality and the vast color range, but you can replace this floss with other brands/colors or overdyed threads if you prefer.

The designs in this book are not large, and most can be stitched in a couple of days or a week or two at the most. I don't personally enjoy projects that take forever to complete (or perhaps I am just lazy!), but many stitchers have also told me they prefer quick-to-stitch pieces because we are all a little time-poor these days.

Each project is accompanied by a full color chart/key and stitching instructions, together with ideas for finishing the piece creatively.

Basic Instructions for Stitching the Designs in This Book

- All designs are stitched over two threads of evenweave fabric (or one block of Aida if you choose to use that material).
- Two threads of embroidery floss are used for cross-stitches, and one thread for backstitch and half stitch.
- French knots are made with one thread of floss, with two wraps around the needle.
- You will need a size 24 or 26 tapestry/cross-stitch needle to stitch these projects, along with a pair of small, sharp embroidery scissors.
- For finishing designs, you will need a pair of larger dressmaking scissors; a sewing machine is helpful but not essential. All of these projects can also be finished using hand sewing.

STITCHES USED

Full Cross-Stitch

Cross-stitch can be worked as a counted stitch over a single square on Aida fabric (shown here) or over two threads when using an evenweave fabric. Each stitch comprises two diagonal stitches that cross in the center. They can be worked individually or in vertical and horizontal rows. Keep the stitches uniform by making sure the top stitch always crosses in the same direction, from upper left to lower right.

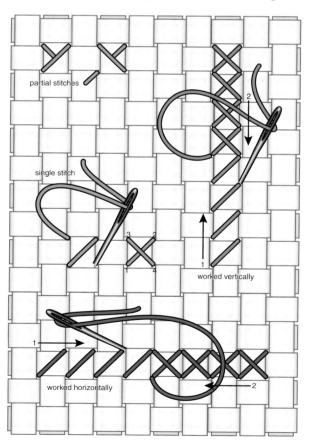

Half Cross-Stitch

Partial cross-stitches may be used where colors abut or along the edges of a design. For a half stitch, work one full diagonal across the square (half the cross).

Backstitch

Backstitch is used to outline a shape and is worked in a motion of two steps forward and one step back. To work the stitch, bring the needle up through the fabric a stitch length's distance from the starting point and insert the needle at the starting point, working the stitch backward. Bring the needle up again a stitch length's distance from the first stitch, and continue working in this manner to the end.

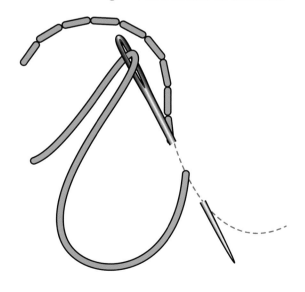

Petite Stitch

A petite stitch is a ¼-size full cross-stitch worked into one of the corners of a square.

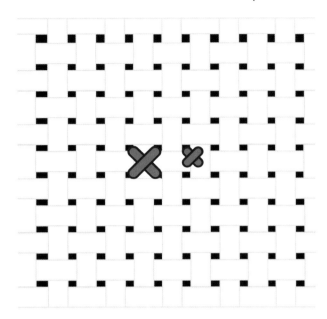

French Knot

Bring the needle up through the fabric, and wrap the working thread around the needle twice. Insert the needle back into the fabric very close to (but not in) the same hole you came out of, and pull the thread through, guiding it with your opposite hand as it passes through the fabric. Do not wrap too tightly, or you'll have a difficult time pulling the needle through the knot. The thread should be against the needle, but not snug or tight. If your knot pulls through to the other side when working the stitch, try loosening the wrap a bit, and make sure you're not going down into the same hole. You will need a bridge to hold the knot on the surface; usually just a fiber or two in the fabric will suffice.

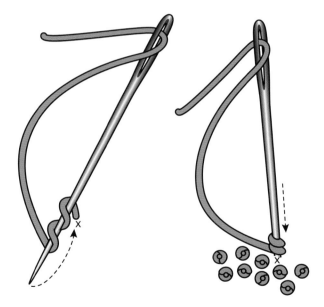

Illustrations and instructions for stitches excerpted from Embroidery Basics *by Cheryl Fall © 2013 Stackpole Books. Used with permission.*

INSPIRE

Little stitched designs and words help us find peace, joy, and hope, especially when we are going through difficult and painful times.

Courage

Someone once said that the only kind of courage we really need sometimes is the kind that gets us from one moment to the next! And by doing so, we can really find our way through even painful or difficult days, one step at a time. Simply by keeping a sense of possibility, of hope, we will begin to see a bigger and better picture for ourselves and our lives and restore ourselves with grace and strength. "Hope is a good thing, perhaps the best of things, and no good thing ever dies." That quote comes from my all-time favorite movie, *The Shawshank Redemption*, and formed the basis of my inspiration for the two designs offered here, both focusing on finding hope and seeing the possibilities—the rainbow!—even on dark and gloomy days.

Keep a Rainbow in Your Sky

This colorful little design reminds us to keep positive and see the blessings and color in every single day! It has been finished as a small, self-standing piece that can be displayed in a number of creative ways in your home; alternatively, it could be framed.

Fabric: 28-count pale blue Jobelan by Wichelt (stitched over 2 threads)
Stitch count: 102 wide × 48 high
Stitched size: 7½ in. (19.1 cm) × 3½ in. (8.9 cm)

Cut the fabric at least 3 inches (7.6 cm) larger than the finished stitching size; fold to find the center, and then count out and start stitching at a convenient point, following the color chart/key. When stitching is completed, wash the piece (if necessary) and press lightly from the back.

Trim the stitched piece to within 1½ inches (3.8 cm) of the stitching all around. Cut two pieces of thin foam core board, each measuring approximately 8 × 4 inches (20.3 × 10.2 cm).

Cover one side of each piece of board with a thin layer of cotton fiberfill or batting, or, alternatively, use a piece of soft felt. Cut a piece of floral or plain cotton fabric, at least 1½ inches (3.8 cm) larger than the foam core board pieces; stretch this piece over the padded side of one of the boards, and glue securely in place at the back. Stretch the stitched piece over the other padded board, and glue this into place at the back too. Spread a layer of glue over the backs of both boards and press them together, fabric and stitched side out. Gently press down with something firm and fairly heavy; leave to dry for at least half an hour. Cut a piece of satin ribbon, at least ⅓ inch (0.8 cm) wide, in a color of your choice, and glue it completely around the two joined pieces, starting and ending at the bottom middle. Then cut another length and make a looped bow (see photo as a guide), and glue it securely in the top middle of the piece. Press in several hat pins (or pins with beaded tops) along the top of the finished piece.

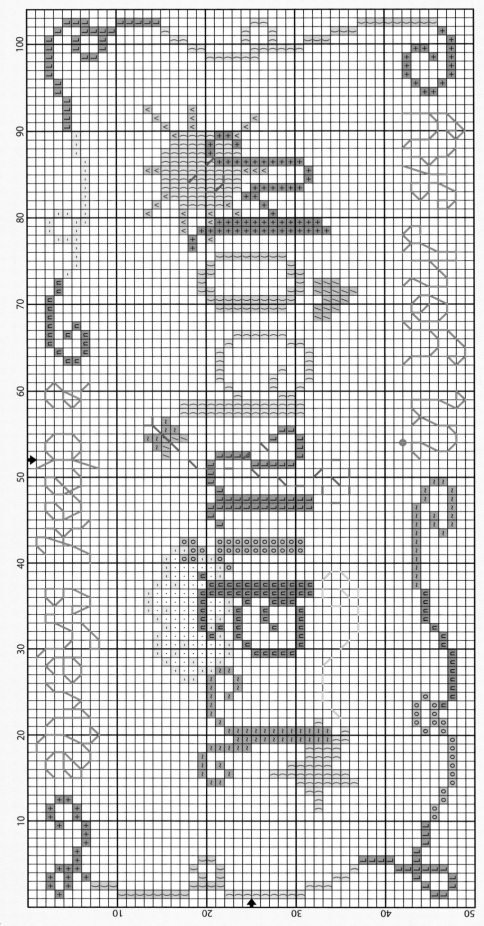

Floss Used for Full Stitches:

Symbol		Strands	Type	Number	Color
	-	2	DMC	415	Pearl Gray
	L	2	DMC	503	Blue Green-MD
	/	2	DMC	760	Salmon
	n	2	DMC	931	Antique Blue-MD
	o	2	DMC	932	Antique Blue-LT
	+	2	DMC	3712	Salmon-MD
	(	2	DMC	3771	Terra Cotta-UL VY LT
	~	2	DMC	3836	Grape-LT
	^	2	DMC	3854	Autumn Gold-MD
	)	2	DMC	3855	Autumn Gold-LT
	·	2	DMC	3865	Winter White

Floss Used for French Knots:

Symbol		Strands	Type	Number	Color
	●	1	DMC	3835	Grape-MD

Floss Used for Back Stitches:

Symbol		Strands	Type	Number	Color
	——	1	DMC	839	Beige Brown-DK
	——	1	DMC	3835	Grape-MD
	——	1	DMC	3854	Autumn Gold-MD

Note:
Stitched on 28-count pale blue Jobelan (by Wichelt), over
2 threads

Hope Is the Song of the Heart

Two happy bluebirds and their little home form the basis of this design, with wording that reminds us to always be hopeful and look for the blessings in our lives. This design was finished as a small pillow with patchwork fabrics and cotton lace, but it could also be simply framed or placed in a hoop.

Fabric: 28-count cafe mocha Country French Linen by Wichelt (stitched over 2 threads)
Stitch count: 63 wide × 63 high
Stitched size: 4½ × 4½ in. (11.4 × 11.4 cm)

You will need a piece of linen at least 9 inches (22.9 cm) square. Fold in half and count out to start stitching at a suitable point. When you have finished stitching, wash and lightly iron the piece on the back (if necessary). Trim the fabric to within 1½ inches (3.8 cm) of the stitching—doing so allows for a ½-inch (1.3-cm) seam when stitching the pillow. Cut two pieces of floral patchwork fabric: one 4½ inches wide × 6½ inches high (11.4 × 16.5 cm), and the other 3¼ inches wide × 6½ inches (8.3 × 16.5 cm) high. Cut a piece of cream cotton lace, and stitch it onto the right side of the larger floral piece, using the photo as a guide. Stitch the two patchwork pieces to the stitched linen piece, right sides together, along the short sides. Press the seams open. Cut a piece of calico or similar fabric the same size as the front pillow piece, and stitch the two pieces together, right sides together, starting at one side and leaving a space of about 3 inches (7.6 cm) for turning/filling. Turn the pillow right side out, press lightly if necessary, and stuff with fiberfill; whipstitch the opening closed.

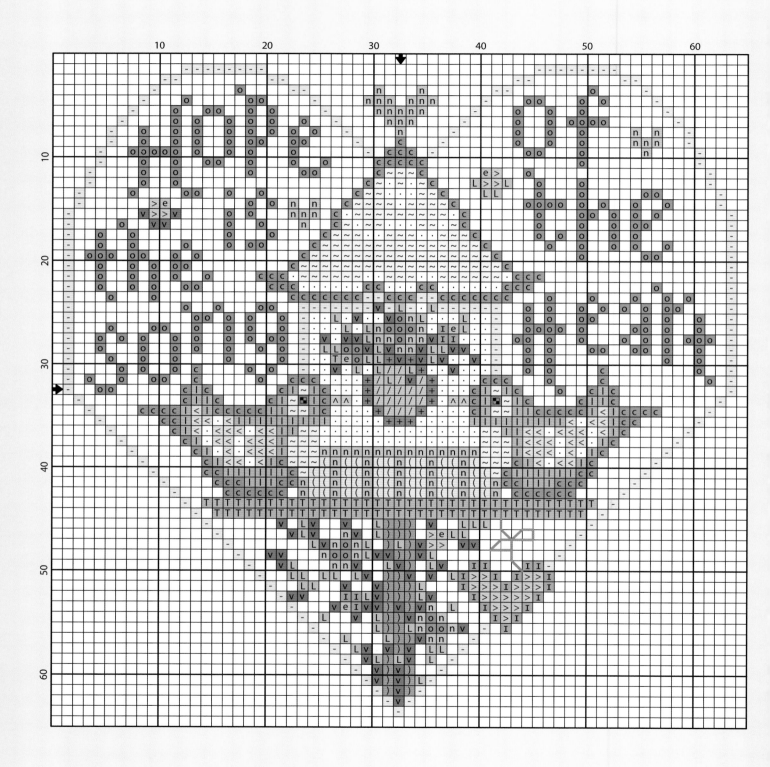

Floss Used for Full Stitches:

	Symbol	Strands	Type	Number	Color
	n	2	DMC	152	Shell Pink-MD LT
	o	2	DMC	223	Shell Pink-LT
	[(	2	DMC	225	Shell Pink-UL VY LT
	I	2	DMC	316	Antique Mauve-MD
	V	2	DMC	502	Blue Green
	+	2	DMC	646	Beaver Gray-DK
	/	2	DMC	647	Beaver Gray-MD
	e	2	DMC	676	Old Gold-LT
	<	2	DMC	754	Peach-LT
	>	2	DMC	778	Antique Mauve-VY LT
	-	2	DMC	822	Beige Gray-LT
	c	2	DMC	926	Gray Green-MD
	I	2	DMC	927	Gray Green-LT
	~	2	DMC	928	Gray Green-VY LT
	)	2	DMC	3032	Mocha Brown-MD
	T	2	DMC	3782	Mocha Brown-LT
	▩	2	DMC	3787	Brown Gray-DK
	L	2	DMC	3813	Blue Green-LT
	^	2	DMC	3827	Golden Brown-Pale
	·	2	DMC	3865	Winter White

Floss Used for Back Stitches:

	Symbol	Strands	Type	Number	Color
	▬▬▬	1	DMC	646	Beaver Gray-DK

Note:
Stitched on 28-count cafe mocha Country French Linen
(by Wichelt), over 2 threads

Self-Esteem

If we have self-esteem, we will always be able to find our way to true happiness and become who we are meant to be; however, if our self-esteem is a little shaky (as is the case for so many of us!), we need to look at developing and maintaining a new and healthy sense of self, no matter what our history or experience might be. It isn't always easy, but it is a vitally important goal. Both of these designs are centered on the idea of "being enough" just as we are: a valuable and important lesson to remind ourselves of every single day as we find our unique and special place in the world.

Just Be You

I think this little pillow is one of my favorite designs in this book because it sends such an important message, and also because it features a darling little sheep—such a charming and underrated animal! Hang this pillow somewhere where you can see its gentle message every day. It also makes a very special gift.

Fabric: 32-count antique white Jobelan by Wichelt (stitched over 2 threads)
Stitch count: 55 wide × 55 high
Stitched size: 4 in. × 4 in. (10.2 × 10.2 cm)

Cut the fabric at least 7 inches (17.8 cm) square; fold in half and count out from the center to start stitching (I find it best to start with the borders, as a rule). When stitching is completed, wash and press the piece (if necessary), and then trim the fabric to measure 5½ inches (14 cm) square (this includes a ½-inch [1.3-cm] seam allowance). Cut a suitable piece of printed cotton fabric to measure the same size, and then pin and stitch the two pieces together, right sides facing, leaving an opening for turning. Turn to the right side and stuff lightly with fiberfill before sewing the opening closed. Cut 2 lengths of ⅓ inch (0.8 cm) satin ribbon, each approximately 12 inches (30.5 cm) in length, and stitch one to each side of the top of the pillow, using the photo as a guide. Add a small button as well, if you like.

Floss Used for Full Stitches:

	Symbol	Strands	Type	Number	Color
	/	2	DMC	522	Fern Green
	0	2	DMC	524	Fern Green-VY LT
	e	2	DMC	640	Beige Gray-VY DK
	>	2	DMC	642	Beige Gray-DK
	-	2	DMC	644	Beige Gray-MD
	V	2	DMC	760	Salmon
	L	2	DMC	761	Salmon-LT
	~	2	DMC	822	Beige Gray-LT
	T	2	DMC	839	Beige Brown-DK
	c	2	DMC	931	Antique Blue-MD
	o	2	DMC	932	Antique Blue-LT
	I	2	DMC	3013	Khaki Green-LT
	n	2	DMC	3053	Green Gray
	l	2	DMC	3752	Antique Blue-VY LT
	(	2	DMC	3753	Antique Blue-UL VY LT
	)	2	DMC	3836	Grape-LT
	^	2	DMC	3855	Autumn Gold-LT
	·	2	DMC	3865	Winter White

Floss Used for French Knots:

	Symbol	Strands	Type	Number	Color
	●	1	DMC	839	Beige Brown-DK
	●	1	DMC	3855	Autumn Gold-LT

Floss Used for Back Stitches:

	Symbol	Strands	Type	Number	Color
	——	1	DMC	839	Beige Brown-DK

Note:
Stitched on 32-count antique white Jobelan
(by Wichelt), over 2 threads

I Am Enough

This is such an important message! I think we should all have this stitched and hanging in our homes. It's also a really easy stitched project, with only a few colors, and should take no more than a couple of days. I have chosen to finish this one simply and inexpensively (but remarkably effectively); you could also frame it, if you prefer.

Fabric: 28-count antique white Jobelan by Wichelt (stitched over 2 threads)
Stitch count: 43 wide × 101 high
Stitched size: 3 in. × 7¾ in. (7.6 × 19.7 cm)

Cut the fabric at least 6 × 11 inches (15.2 × 27.9 cm); fold in half and count out to start stitching at a suitable point. When stitching is complete, wash and lightly press the piece. Trim the piece to within 1 inch (2.5 cm) of the bottom and sides and 2 inches (5.1 cm) from the top. Fold the top over by 1 inch (2.5 cm) and press lightly in place. Take a length of suitable thin ribbon, cord, or similar material; slide it under the folded top, with a matching length at each side; and then tie a small loop in each end for hanging. Hold the ribbon or cord in place with a few tiny clothespins.

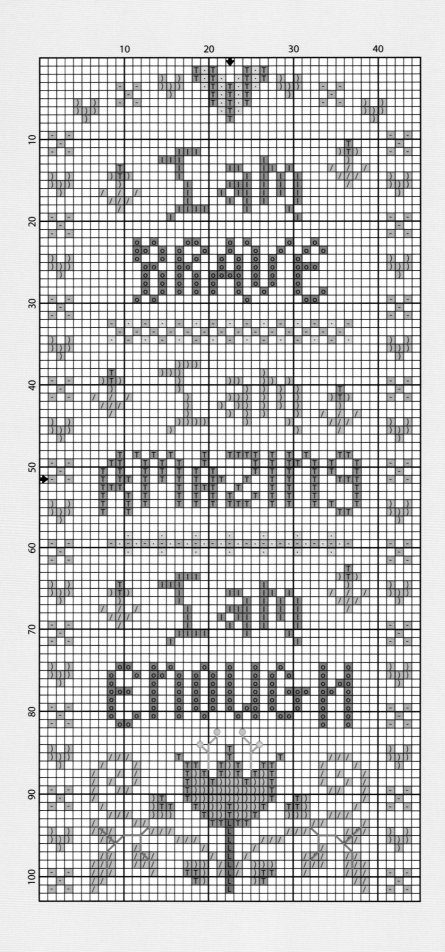

Floss Used for Full Stitches:

Symbol		Strands	Type	Number	Color
■	L	2	DMC	502	Blue Green
□	/	2	DMC	504	Blue Green-LT
□	)	2	DMC	758	Terra Cotta-VY LT
■	I	2	DMC	926	Gray Green-MD
■	-	2	DMC	927	Gray Green-LT
■	o	2	DMC	3768	Gray Green-DK
■	T	2	DMC	3778	Terra Cotta-LT
□	·	2	DMC	3779	Terra Cotta-UL VY LT

Floss Used for French Knots:

Symbol		Strands	Type	Number	Color
□	●	1	DMC	676	Old Gold-LT

Floss Used for Back Stitches:

Symbol		Strands	Type	Number	Color
■	——	1	DMC	502	Blue Green
■	——	1	DMC	3863	Mocha Beige-MD

Note:
Stitched on 28-count antique white Jobelan evenweave
(by Wichelt), over 2 threads

the miracle is here — in this moment in life

Peace

Peace really begins within, and we only find it when we allow ourselves to relax and just "be," without getting caught up in the frantic and often exhausting pace of life today. If we can learn to develop our own quiet oasis of calm, we will be not only happier but also better able to navigate the troubled waters of loss, fear, or conflict. By choosing to place our focus on quiet and mindful moments, we help ourselves heal, grow, and move forward. These two designs (one of which is a miniature mandala, an ancient form of meditation and mindfulness) are designed to remind us that peace is our birthright; it is who we are in our deepest being, and it should be part of our lives on every level—emotional, spiritual, and physical.

The Miracle in the Moment

This moment is all we ever truly have, right here and now—and when we realize this fact, we open our lives up to greater possibilities and joy, for the present is where true magic is to be found.

- -

Fabric: 28-count antique white Jobelan by Wichelt
(stitched over 2 threads)
Stitch count: 59 wide × 83 high
Stitched size: 4 in. × 6 in. (10.2 × 15.2 cm)

Cut fabric at least 7 × 10 inches (17.8 × 25.4 cm); fold in half and count out to start stitching at a convenient point. When stitching is finished, wash and press it (if necessary). This piece was framed in a ready-made frame measuring just over 8 × 10 inches (20.3 × 25.4 cm), with a pale blue mat and an aperture measuring approximately 4¾ × 6½ inches (12.1 × 16.5 cm). I added a small silver owl charm, but that is entirely optional.

Floss Used for Full Stitches:

Symbol		Strands	Type	Number	Color
	o	2	DMC	153	Violet-VY LT
	l	2	DMC	320	Pistachio Green-MD
	-	2	DMC	368	Pistachio Green-LT
	*	2	DMC	413	Pewter Gray-DK
	c	2	DMC	522	Fern Green
	)	2	DMC	524	Fern Green-VY LT
	1	2	DMC	554	Violet-LT
	/	2	DMC	745	Yellow-LT Pale
	L	2	DMC	760	Salmon
	n	2	DMC	761	Salmon-LT
	~	2	DMC	818	Baby Pink
	I	2	DMC	931	Antique Blue-MD
	e	2	DMC	932	Antique Blue-LT
	·	2	DMC	3770	Tawny-VY LT
	(	2	DMC	3832	Raspberry-MD
	V	2	DMC	3855	Autumn Gold-LT
	∧	2	DMC	3863	Mocha Beige-MD

Floss Used for Petite Stitches (ladybug's feet):

Symbol		Strands	Type	Number	Color
	*	2	DMC	413	Pewter Gray-DK

Floss Used for French Knots:

Symbol		Strands	Type	Number	Color
	●	1	DMC	413	Pewter Gray-DK
	●	1	DMC	3855	Autumn Gold-LT

Floss Used for Back Stitches:

Symbol		Strands	Type	Number	Color
	——	1	DMC	413	Pewter Gray-DK
	——	1	DMC	3855	Autumn Gold-LT
	——	1	DMC	3862	Mocha Beige-DK

Note:
Stitched on 28-count antique white Jobelan
(by Wichelt), over 2 threads

Little Peace Garden Mandala

Mandalas (the word comes from Sanskrit and means "circle") are an ancient form of artwork and meditation, reputed to bring a sense of calm and mindfulness. This is a simple and colorful little stitched mandala that will surely imbue us with peace as we stitch the gentle repeating patterns.

Fabric: 32-count antique white Belfast Linen by Zweigart (stitched over 2 threads)
Stitch count: 47 wide × 47 high
Approximate size: 3 in. (7.6 cm) diameter

Cut the selected fabric at least 5½ inches (14 cm) square. Fold in half and count out to begin stitching at a suitable place. When stitching is complete, lightly press the piece (if necessary). The mandala is mounted in a 4-inch (10.2-cm) wooden hoop; trim the fabric into a circle measuring 5 inches (12.7 cm) across, and then insert the stitching into the hoop, ensuring the design is centered and smooth. Tighten the hoop, and then fold the excess fabric to the back; you can stitch or glue it down if necessary. I usually cut a circle of felt that is just the same size as the outer ring of the hoop and glue it in place on the back of the hoop to cover the back of the stitching. Cut a length of satin ribbon in a color of your choice, and tie it through the top of the hoop to make a hanging.

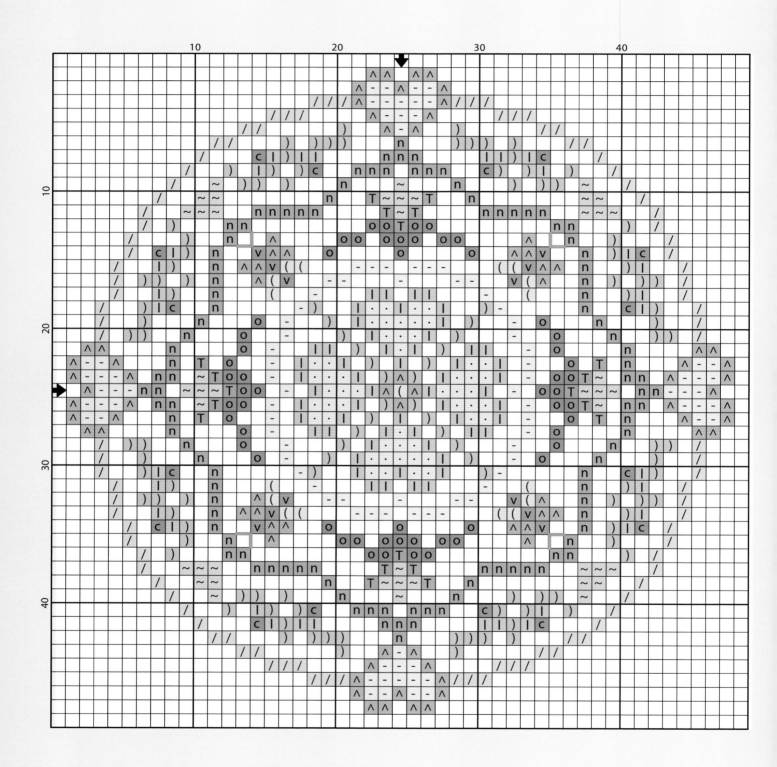

Floss Used for Full Stitches:

Symbol		Strands	Type	Number	Color
	I	2	DMC	152	Shell Pink-MD LT
	c	2	DMC	223	Shell Pink-LT
	·	2	DMC	225	Shell Pink-UL VY LT
	T	2	DMC	316	Antique Mauve-MD
	)	2	DMC	368	Pistachio Green-LT
	o	2	DMC	522	Fern Green
	/	2	DMC	524	Fern Green-VY LT
	-	2	DMC	822	Beige Gray-LT
	v	2	DMC	3032	Mocha Brown-MD
	^	2	DMC	3042	Antique Violet-LT
	n	2	DMC	3364	Pine Green
	~	2	DMC	3727	Antique Mauve-LT
	(	2	DMC	3855	Autumn Gold-LT

Floss Used for Back Stitches:

Symbol		Strands	Type	Number	Color
	————	1	DMC	3032	Mocha Brown-MD

Note:
Stitched on 32-count antique white Belfast
Linen (by Zweigart), over 2 threads

Serenity

Many people think serenity is just another word for peace, but I believe it is a unique way of finding a path to a more joyful and mindful life as we open ourselves to the simple beauty around us, every day. In this way we can discover a new way of looking at and experiencing our lives—sometimes by doing something as simple as taking the time to breathe, slowly and with awareness. There is always something to remind us of the blessings of life, even on dark days and in difficult times, and these two designs gently remind us of that.

Beautiful Day

The little songbird and owl on this colorful hanging remind us that every day can be good and blessed if we just open our eyes and our hearts!

Fabric: 28-count antique white Jobelan by Wichelt (stitched over 2 threads)
Stitch count: 53 wide × 113 high
Stitched size: 3¾ in. wide × 8¼ in. high (9.5 × 21 cm)

Cut the fabric at least 6 inches wide × 11 inches high (15.2 × 27.9 cm); the extra is needed for creating the hanging at the top. Fold in half and count out to start stitching at a convenient point. When the stitching is completed, wash and press the piece (if necessary), and trim any frayed edges. Fold in the sides so that they measure about ½ inch (1.3 cm) away from the embroidered edge, and then hemstitch in place on the wrong side, using cotton thread. Fold and stitch the bottom edge in the same way, ensuring that the corners are neatly folded and stitched to the back.

Fold down the top, leaving a space of at least ¾ inch (1.9 cm) for the dowel/stick for hanging, and stitch in place neatly. Slide through a dowel (I used a small stick from my garden) measuring 7 inches (17.8 cm) in length. Tie a narrow ribbon on one side of the hanging and then carry it across and tie it on the other side, leaving a loop at least 14 inches (35.6 cm) long. You can also add a length of fine lace on each side, as shown in the picture.

Floss Used for Full Stitches:

Symbol		Strands	Type	Number	Color
	n	2	DMC	152	Shell Pink-MD LT
	v	2	DMC	223	Shell Pink-LT
	<	2	DMC	225	Shell Pink-UL VY LT
	o	2	DMC	316	Antique Mauve-MD
	+	2	DMC	356	Terra Cotta-MD
	I	2	DMC	522	Fern Green
	((	2	DMC	524	Fern Green-VY LT
	S	2	DMC	839	Beige Brown-DK
	T	2	DMC	926	Gray Green-MD
	/	2	DMC	927	Gray Green-LT
	-	2	DMC	3042	Antique Violet-LT
	L	2	DMC	3053	Green Gray
	I	2	DMC	3727	Antique Mauve-LT
	>	2	DMC	3771	Terra Cotta-UL VY LT
	m	2	DMC	3854	Autumn Gold-MD
	c	2	DMC	3855	Autumn Gold-LT
	∧	2	DMC	3862	Mocha Beige-DK
	~	2	DMC	3864	Mocha Beige-LT
	·	2	DMC	3865	Winter White

Floss Used for French Knots:

Symbol		Strands	Type	Number	Color
	●	1	DMC	223	Shell Pink-LT
	●	1	DMC	839	Beige Brown-DK

Floss Used for Back Stitches:

Symbol		Strands	Type	Number	Color
	———	1	DMC	356	Terra Cotta-MD
	———	1	DMC	839	Beige Brown-DK
	———	1	DMC	926	Gray Green-MD
	———	1	DMC	3854	Autumn Gold-MD
	———	1	DMC	3862	Mocha Beige-DK

Note:
Stitched on 28-count antique white Jobelan (by Wichelt),
over 2 threads

Let Go and Breathe

Let go and breathe . . . something to remember, each and every day—it's the way to bring calm, clarity, and peace into our lives. This is such a simple project, done in just three colors; of course, you can swap out the blue linen for another shade and stitch the words in your own personal color preference. Although I have also finished this project as a simple hanging piece, it could be framed or stitched up as a small pillow, if preferred.

Fabric: 28-count rain Country French Linen by Wichelt
(stitched over 2 threads)
Stitch count: 71 wide × 71 high
Stitched size: 5 × 5 in. (12.7 × 12.7 cm)

Cut fabric at least 8 inches (20.3 cm) square, and then fold in half and count out to start stitching at a suitable point. When stitching is complete, press the work (if necessary), and then trim it to 6 inches (15.2 cm) square at the sides and bottom and 7 inches (17.8 cm) at the top. Finish the piece as a simple hanging, using the instructions given for "I Am Enough" on page 20.

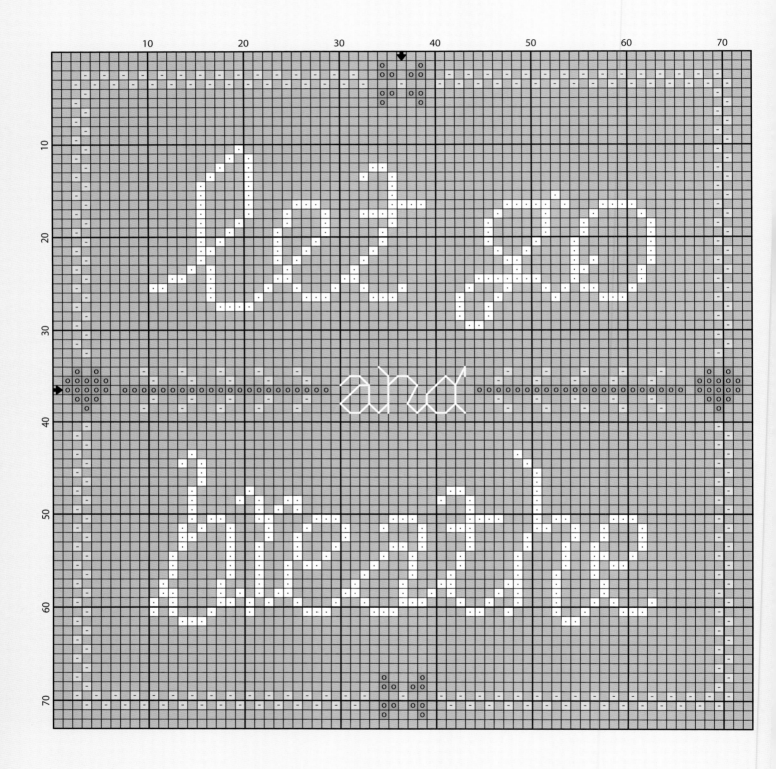

Floss Used for Full Stitches:

Symbol		Strands	Type	Number	Color
▨	o	2	DMC	932	Antique Blue-LT
▢	-	2	DMC	3752	Antique Blue-VY LT
□	·	2	DMC	3865	Winter White

Floss Used for Back Stitches:

Symbol	Strands	Type	Number	Color
□	1	DMC	3865	Winter White

Note:
Stitched on 28-count rain Country French Linen (by Wichelt), over 2 threads

Joy

Joy is our birthright, a deep and lasting sense of
happiness that can fill and enrich our lives and
relationships on a daily basis; it's the ultimate result of
knowing, loving, and accepting ourselves and others
in the world around us. Real joy makes us whole and
healthy, and it is always a choice we can make, even
when things seem really dark and hopeless. Let us
remember to look up, lift our hearts, and smile, as these
two designs remind us. And let us also remember to eat
cake . . . preferably chocolate, of course!

Choose Joy Today

I love this softly colored piece, simply and effectively mounted in a wooden hoop. Hang it anywhere you would like to have a positive and uplifting message for your day!

Fabric: 32-count latte Country French Linen by Wichelt (stitched over 2 threads)
Stitch count: 71 wide × 71 high
Stitched size: 4¼ in (10.8 cm) diameter

Cut the fabric at least 9 inches (22.9 cm) in diameter, and then fold in half and count out to start stitching at a suitable point. When the stitching is complete, wash and press the work (if necessary), and then trim into a circle measuring at least 8 inches (20.3 cm) in diameter. Insert into a 6-inch (15.2-cm) wooden hoop, and finish following the instructions for "Little Peace Garden Mandala" on page 30.

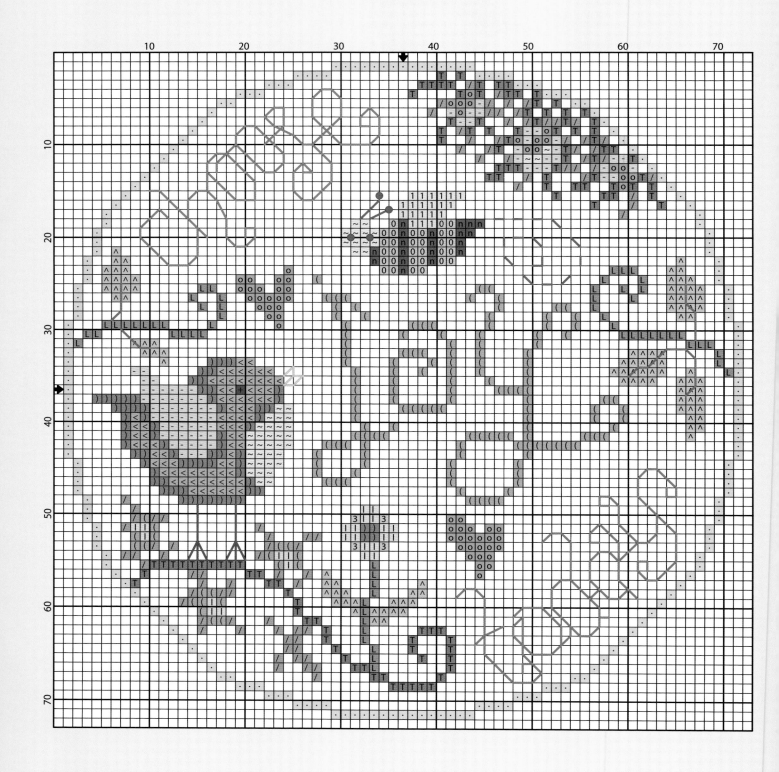

Floss Used for Full Stitches:

Symbol		Strands	Type	Number	Color
	T	2	DMC	522	Fern Green
	/	2	DMC	523	Fern Green-LT
	·	2	DMC	524	Fern Green-VY LT
	0	2	DMC	676	Old Gold-LT
	+	2	DMC	839	Beige Brown-DK
	~	2	DMC	950	Desert Sand-LT
	^	2	DMC	3013	Khaki Green-LT
	(	2	DMC	3042	Antique Violet-LT
	1	2	DMC	3072	Beaver Gray-VY LT
	L	2	DMC	3364	Pine Green
	o	2	DMC	3778	Terra Cotta-LT
	-	2	DMC	3779	Terra Cotta-UL VY LT
	n	2	DMC	3787	Brown Gray-DK
	3	2	DMC	3827	Golden Brown-Pale
	l	2	DMC	3855	Autumn Gold-LT
	)	2	DMC	3863	Mocha Beige-MD
	<	2	DMC	3864	Mocha Beige-LT

Floss Used for French Knots:

Symbol		Strands	Type	Number	Color
	●	1	DMC	3787	Brown Gray-DK

Floss Used for Back Stitches:

Symbol		Strands	Type	Number	Color
	——	1	DMC	839	Beige Brown-DK
	——	1	DMC	3041	Antique Violet-MD
	——	1	DMC	3363	Pine Green-MD
	——	1	DMC	3787	Brown Gray-DK
	——	1	DMC	3827	Golden Brown-Pale

Note:
Stitched on 32-count latte Country French Linen (by Wichelt),
over 2 threads

Little Angel Mantra

I believe angels—those we can see and those we can't—are always present in our lives, and I also believe they want us to be the truly happy, joyful, and peaceful beings that they are! It starts with simplicity and enjoying the quiet and real pleasures of our days: life, the love around us, and, of course, cake! This is a fun little piece in pretty colors and will surely brighten your day or a loved one's.

Fabric: 28-count antique white Lugana by Zweigart (stitched over 2 threads)
Stitch count: 92 wide × 52 high
Stitched size: 6½ × 3½ in. (16.5 × 8.9 cm)

Cut fabric at least 10 inches wide by 6 inches high (25.4 × 15.2 cm); fold in half and count out to start stitching at a suitable point. When stitching is completed, wash and press the piece (if necessary), and then trim the piece to measure 8 inches wide by 5½ inches high (20.3 × 14 cm).

Cut a piece of thin foam core board measuring 7 × 4 inches (17.8 × 10.2 cm) and cover with a piece of thin batting or felt, and then glue into place. Center the stitched piece on the board and wrap edges of fabric to the back; glue in place very well. Cut another piece of foam core board measuring 8 inches by 5 inches (20.3 × 12.7 cm), and cover with a piece of cotton patchwork fabric in a suitable color/print; fold this fabric to the back, glue in place, and then cover the back with a piece of felt cut to fit and glued on. Finally, glue a loop of ribbon to either side of the stitched and mounted piece (see photo for a guide), and then glue this down onto the fabric side of the larger board. Press down firmly until they are completely dry.

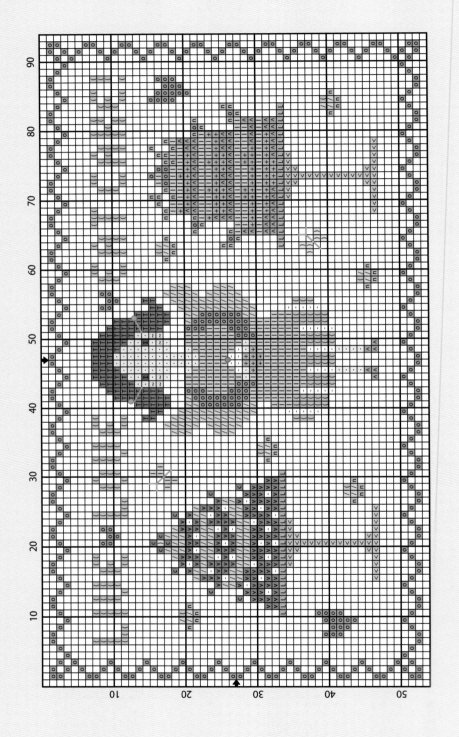

Floss Used for Full Stitches:

Symbol		Strands	Type	Number	Color
	(	2	DMC	210	Lavender-MD
	/	2	DMC	211	Lavender-LT
	n	2	DMC	368	Pistachio Green-LT
	^	2	DMC	436	Tan
	+	2	DMC	437	Tan-LT
	c	2	DMC	553	Violet
	L	2	DMC	642	Beige Gray-DK
	<	2	DMC	644	Beige Gray-MD
	)	2	DMC	744	Yellow-Pale
	~	2	DMC	754	Peach-LT
	I	2	DMC	838	Beige Brown-VY DK
	·	2	DMC	948	Peach-VY LT
	o	2	DMC	3688	Mauve-MD
	I	2	DMC	3689	Mauve-LT
	T	2	DMC	3790	Beige Gray-UL DK
	v	2	DMC	3862	Mocha Beige-DK
	-	2	DMC	3865	Winter White

Floss Used for French Knots:

Symbol		Strands	Type	Number	Color
	●	1	DMC	553	Violet
	●	1	DMC	3688	Mauve-MD

Floss Used for Back Stitches:

Symbol		Strands	Type	Number	Color
	——	1	DMC	436	Tan
	——	1	DMC	3688	Mauve-MD

Note:
Stitched on 28-count antique white Lugana (by Zweigart),
over 2 threads

2

CREATE

This section reminds us just how powerful and necessary it is for human beings to be creative; it is part of who we are, and, more powerfully, creativity is not only wonderfully relaxing and enjoyable but also truly healing. Who among us has not found peace and calm when working on a creative project of any kind? These designs focus on different aspects of creativity and how we can empower and enrich ourselves through the simple art of making—be it something concrete like a stitched sampler, a flower garden, or a cake—or something more intangible, like a greater sense of courage and self.

Begin
Go with Your Heart
A New Journey

Dream
Dream Big
Make Your Dreams Real

Believe
Write from the Heart
The Beauty You Love

Grow
Bloom!
Lovely Day Angel

Passion
Live Your Passion
Do It with Heart

Begin

Sometimes beginning something new can seem overwhelming and even frightening, especially if it's something we haven't tried before—whether it's a new recipe, stitching a quilt, moving to a new place, or changing one's whole life! But the simple act of beginning can have enormous power to increase our self-confidence and belief that we can do it: it doesn't matter how small the start; it's the stepping forward that counts!

Go with Your Heart

This little heart-shaped piece (and wise owl!) reminds us that our heart always prompts us in the right direction if we just listen to it and take that first step.

Fabric: 28-count antique white Jobelan by Wichelt (stitched over 2 threads)

Stitch count: 71 wide × 75 high

Approximate finished size: 5 × 5¼ in. (12.7 × 13.3 cm)

Cut the fabric to measure at least 8 × 8 inches (20.3 × 20.3 cm); fold in half and count out from the center to start stitching at a convenient point. When the stitching is completed, wash and lightly iron the piece.

To make up this design as a freestanding piece (as shown), please follow the instructions for "Keep a Rainbow in Your Sky" on page 6. However, you will need to cut 2 pieces of foam core board that each measure 6 × 6 inches (15.2 × 15.2 cm), and cover one with a matching piece of light batting or felt. The other is covered with a piece of patchwork/floral fabric measuring approximately 7 × 7 inches (17.8 × 17.8 cm).

Floss Used for Full Stitches:

Symbol		Strands	Type	Number	Color
■	n	2	DMC	223	Shell Pink-LT
□	-	2	DMC	224	Shell Pink-VY LT
□	)	2	DMC	368	Pistachio Green-LT
■	∧	2	DMC	522	Fern Green
□	(	2	DMC	524	Fern Green-VY LT
■	0	2	DMC	640	Beige Gray-VY DK
□	¬	2	DMC	778	Antique Mauve-VY LT
■	o	2	DMC	926	Gray Green-MD
■	I	2	DMC	927	Gray Green-LT
□	~	2	DMC	928	Gray Green-VY LT
□	L	2	DMC	3042	Antique Violet-LT
□	v	2	DMC	3364	Pine Green
□	>	2	DMC	3827	Golden Brown-Pale
□	/	2	DMC	3855	Autumn Gold-LT
■	c	2	DMC	3863	Mocha Beige-MD
□	<	2	DMC	3864	Mocha Beige-LT
□	·	2	DMC	3865	Winter White

Floss Used for Half Stitches (doorway and window):

Symbol		Strands	Type	Number	Color
■	0	2	DMC	640	Beige Gray-VY DK

Floss Used for Back Stitches:

Symbol		Strands	Type	Number	Color
■	▬	1	DMC	640	Beige Gray-VY DK
□		1	DMC	3865	Winter White

Note:
Stitched on 28-count antique white Jobelan
(by Wichelt), over 2 threads

A New Journey

Life takes us on many journeys—each one requiring a new beginning and leap of faith—but if we trust in the magic of the journey and where it is leading us, we will find new possibilities, joy, and magic! After all, I believe that there are no journeys that don't take us somewhere we need to be for our personal growth and happiness.

Fabric: 28-count antique white Jobelan by Wichelt (stitched over two threads)
Stitch count: 39 wide × 101 high
Approximate size: 2¾ × 7¼ in. (7 × 18.4 cm)

Cut the fabric at least 5 × 13 inches (12.7 × 33 cm); fold in half and count out to start stitching at a suitable point. When you have finished, wash and lightly press the piece on the wrong side. Trim the fabric to within 1 inch (2.5 cm) at the sides of the piece, 1 inch (2.5 cm) at the bottom, and 3 inches (7.6 cm) at the top (you need more fabric at the top for the fold over). Stitch a small hem all around the piece, using a matching thread. Fold the top down to fit over a small wooden hanger, as shown, and catch in place at the sides.

Tie a narrow length of satin ribbon from one side of the hanger to the other for hanging. You can also add beads (as I did) to each side of the hanging at the bottom, or even small tassels.

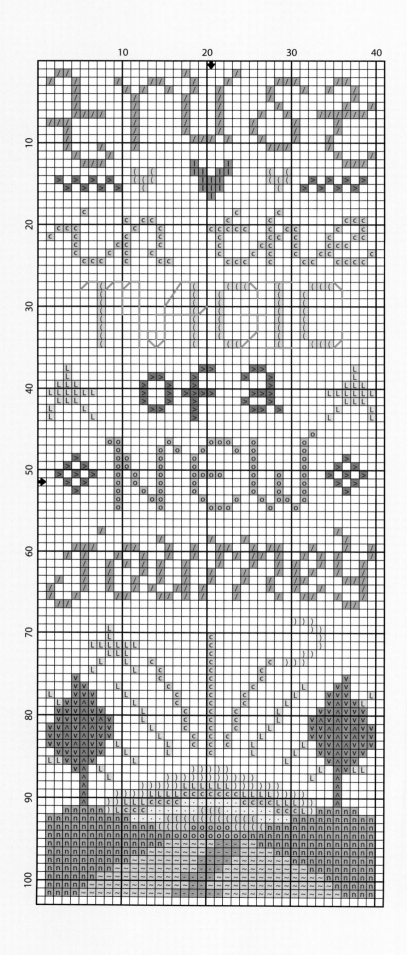

Floss Used for Full Stitches:

Symbol		Strands	Type	Number	Color
▢	v	2	DMC	522	Fern Green
▢	n	2	DMC	646	Beaver Gray-DK
▢	)	2	DMC	745	Yellow-LT Pale
▢	o	2	DMC	760	Salmon
▢	(	2	DMC	761	Salmon-LT
▢	>	2	DMC	931	Antique Blue-MD
▢	/	2	DMC	932	Antique Blue-LT
▢	~	2	DMC	3024	Brown Gray-VY LT
▢	-	2	DMC	3032	Mocha Brown-MD
▢	I	2	DMC	3712	Salmon-MD
▢	·	2	DMC	3713	Salmon-VY LT
▢	c	2	DMC	3827	Golden Brown-Pale
▢	L	2	DMC	3855	Autumn Gold-LT
▢	^	2	DMC	3862	Mocha Beige-DK

Floss Used for Back Stitches:

Symbol		Strands	Type	Number	Color
▢	———	1	DMC	3712	Salmon-MD

Note:
Stitched on 28-count antique white Jobelan
(by Wichelt), over 2 threads

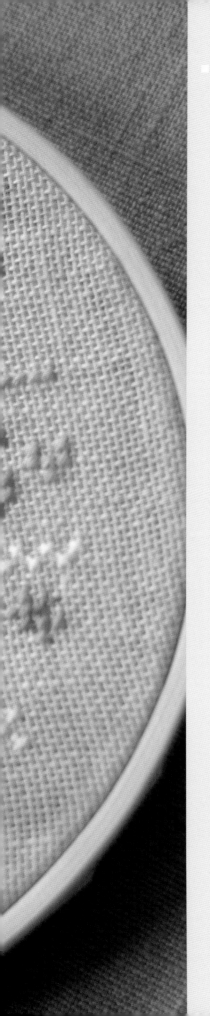

Dream

Dreams are one of the most powerful forces available to us. After all, as someone once said, nothing happens unless we first dream it! I think we need to honor and listen to our dreams—even if they seem a little unrealistic or out of reach (and especially if they seem quite impossible!). Nothing is impossible in this life if we are brave enough to hang in and stay the course.

Dream Big

This piece, with its row of colorful and unconventional sheep, reminds us that starting small is perfectly acceptable, and it can ultimately lead to the accomplishment of really big and special dreams.

- -

Fabric: 28-count star sapphire Jobelan by Wichelt
(stitched over 2 threads)
Stitch count: 107 wide × 55 high
Approximate size: 7½ × 4¼ in. (19.1 × 10.8 cm)

Cut the fabric at least 11 × 8 inches (27.9 × 20.3 cm); fold in half and count out to start stitching at a convenient point. When you have completed the stitching, wash and iron the piece lightly. This design is not presented in a finished form because there are a number of options: it would make a lovely framed piece, or it could also be finished as a freestanding piece (see "Go with Your Heart" on page 58) or as a pillow with or without fabric borders.

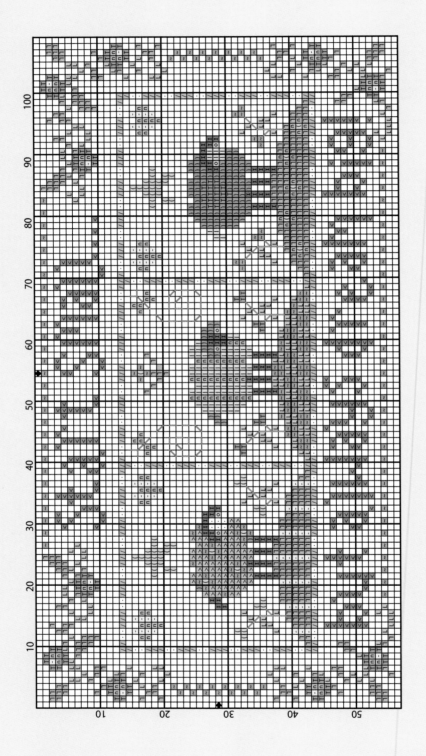

Floss Used for Full Stitches:

	Symbol	Strands	Type	Number	Color
	n	2	DMC	152	Shell Pink-MD LT
	T	2	DMC	223	Shell Pink-LT
	-	2	DMC	225	Shell Pink-UL VY LT
	<	2	DMC	316	Antique Mauve-MD
	˥	2	DMC	524	Fern Green-VY LT
	I	2	DMC	640	Beige Gray-VY DK
	)	2	DMC	642	Beige Gray-DK
	>	2	DMC	644	Beige Gray-MD
	/	2	DMC	778	Antique Mauve-VY LT
	I	2	DMC	822	Beige Gray-LT
	~	2	DMC	3042	Antique Violet-LT
	L	2	DMC	3364	Pine Green
	o	2	DMC	3779	Terra Cotta-UL VY LT
	(	2	DMC	3855	Autumn Gold-LT
	·	2	DMC	3865	Winter White

Floss Used for Back Stitches:

	Symbol	Strands	Type	Number	Color
	——————	1	DMC	640	Beige Gray-VY DK
	——————	1	DMC	3363	Pine Green-MD

Note:
Stitched on 28-count star sapphire Jobelan
(by Wichelt), over 2 threads

Make Your Dreams Real

The concept of the dreamcatcher in traditional wisdom and folklore has always seemed both powerful and comforting: in the night, the dreamcatcher gently retains the important and beautiful dreams while carefully blowing away those that are less helpful to us. I wanted to create a small, stitched dreamcatcher to honor this lovely tradition.

Fabric: 28-count mocha Country French Linen by Wichelt (stitched over 2 threads)
Stitch count: 57 wide × 57 high
Approximate size: 4 × 4 in. (10.2 × 10.2 cm)

Cut the fabric at least 7 × 7 inches (17.8 × 17.8 cm); fold in half and count out to start stitching at a suitable point. When the stitching is complete, wash and lightly iron the piece. To complete the dreamcatcher, you will need a wooden embroidery hoop measuring around 5¼ inches (13.3 cm) in diameter. Remove the inner hoop and tie several small ribbons/pieces of lace at the bottom of the outer hoop, using the photo as a guide. (You can also stitch on beads, charms, or even small feathers, if you like.) Trim the embroidered piece to measure around 6 inches (15.2 cm) in diameter, and fold it around the inner hoop, ensuring that it is centered. Insert the outer hoop and tighten, pulling the fabric to the back so the design is flat and smooth. Cover the back of the hoop with a piece of fabric or felt cut to fit. Attach a length of ribbon to the top of the dreamcatcher for hanging.

Floss Used for Full Stitches:

Symbol		Strands	Type	Number	Color
	o	2	DMC	152	Shell Pink-MD LT
	-	2	DMC	223	Shell Pink-LT
	/	2	DMC	225	Shell Pink-UL VY LT
	n	2	DMC	316	Antique Mauve-MD
	v	2	DMC	522	Fern Green
	l	2	DMC	524	Fern Green-VY LT
	L	2	DMC	778	Antique Mauve-VY LT
	~	2	DMC	3032	Mocha Brown-MD
	)	2	DMC	3042	Antique Violet-LT
	>	2	DMC	3053	Green Gray
	[	2	DMC	3855	Autumn Gold-LT
	c	2	DMC	3856	Mahogany-UL VY LT
	·	2	DMC	3865	Winter White

Floss Used for Back Stitches:

Symbol		Strands	Type	Number	Color
	————	1	DMC	3787	Brown Gray-DK

Note:
Stitched on 28-count mocha Country French Linen
(by Wichelt), over 2 threads

Believe

Belief—both in ourselves and in what we do—is a vital part of the creative process, but it is also unfortunately something that many of us struggle with! Overcome disbelief with reminders to trust yourself and your unique and special abilities and talents.

Write from the Heart

One way of overcoming creative blocks is to keep a journal—a safe space where you can express your hopes, plans, and ideas, no matter how far-fetched they may seem. And creating a beautiful hand-stitched cover for your journal makes it even more special!

Fabric: 28-count latte Country French Linen by Wichelt (stitched over 2 threads)
Stitch count: 69 wide × 95 high
Approximate size: 5½ × 6¾ in. (14 × 17.2 cm)

This design was created to fit over a softcover journal measuring approximately 6 × 8 inches (15.2 × 20.3 cm); however, it can be adapted to fit a slightly smaller or larger journal simply by adjusting the fabric size. You will need to have a piece of fabric large enough to wrap around the journal on both sides, with at least 3 inches (7.6 cm) on each short end (for the flaps for the book to tuck into) and at least 2 inches (5.1 cm) on both the top and the bottom edges. Then fold the fabric in half, center the design on the top half, and start stitching at a convenient point.

When you have finished stitching, wash and press the piece so it lies flat; trim any raw or frayed edges. Lay the fabric on the book and work a hem all around with small running stitches in a matching thread color. For each end, fold up about 1½ inches (3.8 cm) to form a flap, and hold it in place with a few stitches on each side. Insert the journal into the cover, with front and back covers held in place by the flaps. Stitch two lengths of ribbon in the middle of the front/back covers and tie the journal closed.

Floss Used for Full Stitches:

Symbol		Strands	Type	Number	Color
	/	2	DMC	152	Shell Pink-MD LT
	I	2	DMC	223	Shell Pink-LT
	·	2	DMC	225	Shell Pink-UL VY LT
	L	2	DMC	316	Antique Mauve-MD
	-	2	DMC	778	Antique Mauve-VY LT
	n	2	DMC	3363	Pine Green-MD
	((	2	DMC	3364	Pine Green
	o	2	DMC	3722	Shell Pink-MD

Note:
Stitched on 28-count latte Country French Linen
(by Wichelt), over 2 threads

The Beauty You Love

This little stitched pillow has a mantra that reminds us to trust in our own innate creativity and to bring it forth to share it with the world!

Fabric: 28-count China pearl Jobelan by Wichelt (stitched over 2 threads)

Stitch count: 53 wide × 37 high

Approximate size: 3¾ × 2½ in. (9.5 × 6.4 cm)

You will need a piece of fabric at least 6 × 7 inches (15.2 × 17.8 cm); fold in half and count out to start stitching at a suitable point. When the stitching is finished, wash and press the piece, and trim it carefully to 1½ inches (3.8 cm) around the stitched area. Cut a piece of cotton fabric to the same size, place the two rectangles together (right sides facing), and stitch around the pillow with a ½-inch (1.3-cm) seam, leaving a small gap at the bottom. (Stitch in a loop of ribbon at the center top for hanging.)

Turn the piece right side out, stuff lightly with fiberfill, and slip stitch the opening closed. Stitch a small button on top of the ribbon hanger.

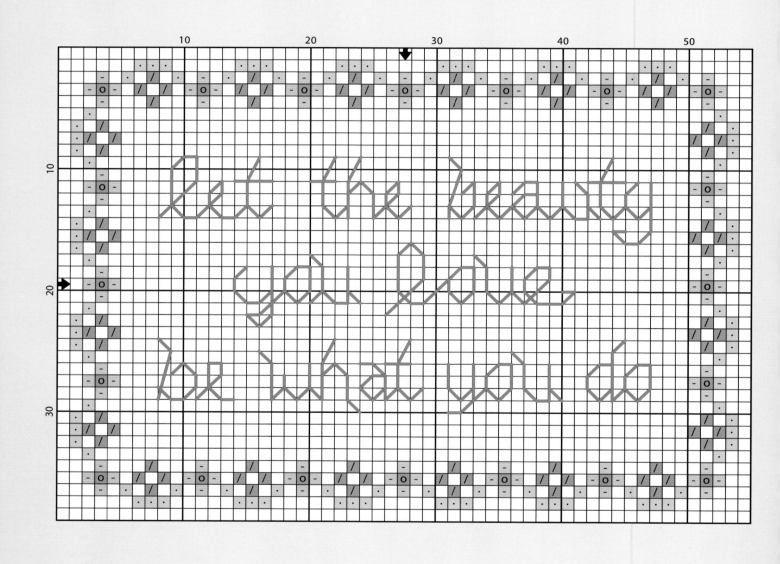

Floss Used for Full Stitches:

Symbol		Strands	Type	Number	Color
▨	o	2	DMC	316	Antique Mauve-MD
▨	-	2	DMC	778	Antique Mauve-VY LT
▨	/	2	DMC	927	Gray Green-LT
▨	·	2	DMC	928	Gray Green-VY LT

Floss Used for Back Stitches:

Symbol		Strands	Type	Number	Color
▨	————	1	DMC	3726	Antique Mauve-DK

Note:
Stitched on 28-count China pearl Jobelan
(by Wichelt), over 2 threads

Grow

Creativity is, in and of itself, one of the ways we grow and develop on every level; when we create things, we tap into our "happy" space and bloom, much as a flower does when planted in the right soil and given plenty of water and sunlight!

Bloom!

This is a bright and happy piece, similar to a mandala; it reminds us that we also have the power to bloom and grow, no matter who and where we are—we can be the wonderful, bright, and creative beings we are meant to be.

Fabric: 28-count waterlily Jobelan by Wichelt (stitched over 2 threads)
Stitch count: 69 wide × 69 high
Approximate size: 5 × 5 in. (12.7 cm)

Cut the fabric to measure at least 9 × 9 inches (22.9 × 22.9 cm); fold in half and count out to start stitching at a convenient point. When stitching is complete, wash and lightly press the piece. You will need a 6-inch (15.2-cm) wooden hoop; remove the outer ring and measure the stitched piece over the inner hoop. Carefully trim the fabric in a circle approximately 1 inch (2.5 cm) larger than the hoop, and then stretch and secure it in place with the outer hoop, making sure the design is centered. Add a length of ribbon at the top of the hoop for hanging.

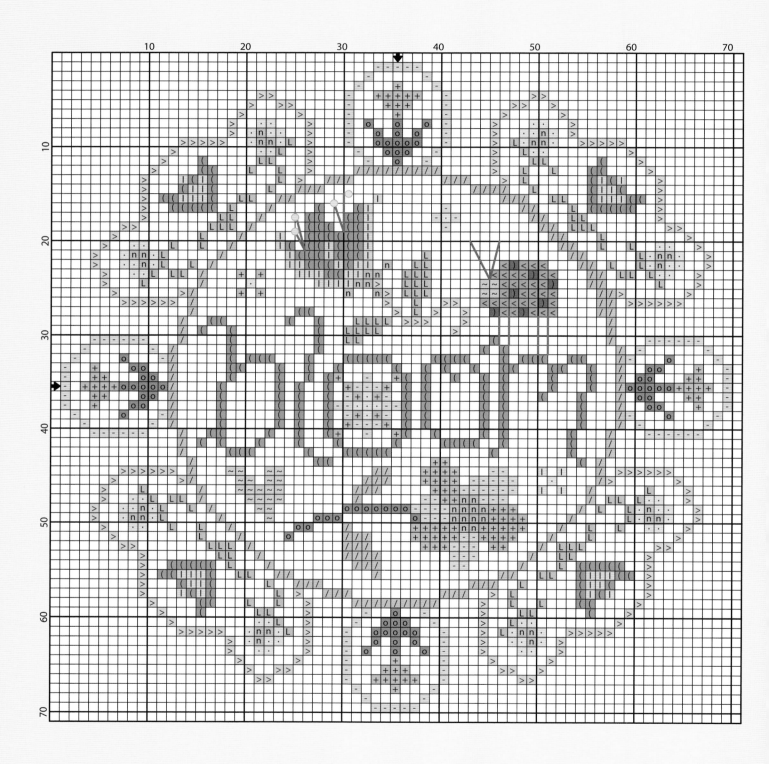

Floss Used for Full Stitches:

Symbol		Strands	Type	Number	Color
	I	2	DMC	153	Violet-VY LT
	L	2	DMC	368	Pistachio Green-LT
	n	2	DMC	436	Tan
	o	2	DMC	522	Fern Green
	/	2	DMC	524	Fern Green-VY LT
	~	2	DMC	758	Terra Cotta-VY LT
	+	2	DMC	760	Salmon
	-	2	DMC	761	Salmon-LT
	>	2	DMC	3053	Green Gray
	<	2	DMC	3712	Salmon-MD
	)	2	DMC	3787	Brown Gray-DK
	(	2	DMC	3836	Grape-LT
	·	2	DMC	3855	Autumn Gold-LT

Floss Used for French Knots:

Symbol		Strands	Type	Number	Color
	●	1	DMC	3855	Autumn Gold-LT

Floss Used for Back Stitches:

Symbol		Strands	Type	Number	Color
	——	1	DMC	3787	Brown Gray-DK

Note:
Stitched on 28-count waterlily Jobelan
(by Wichelt), over 2 threads

Lovely Day Angel

It's always possible to create our own happy days and joy—in fact, it's essential! And this bright angel, with her colorful knitting and happy little canine companion, reminds us that creativity is a good place to start.

Fabric: 28-count antique white Jobelan by Wichelt (stitched over 2 threads)

Stitch count: 58 wide × 74 high

Approximate size: 5¼ × 6¼ in. (13.3 × 15.9 cm)

Cut the fabric to measure at least 8 × 10 inches (20.3 × 25.4 cm); fold in half and count out to start stitching at a convenient point. When the stitching is done, wash and lightly iron the piece. Trim the edges neatly and iron a small fold in the top of the fabric. Pass a length of ribbon or cord through the fold, and hold in place with a few mini clothespins; this method makes a simple and effective finishing of the piece, which can then be hung up to add a colorful message anywhere!

Floss Used for Full Stitches:

Symbol		Strands	Type	Number	Color
▢	v	2	DMC	320	Pistachio Green-MD
▢	)	2	DMC	368	Pistachio Green-LT
▢	^	2	DMC	434	Brown-LT
▢	c	2	DMC	436	Tan
▢	l	2	DMC	554	Violet-LT
▢	(	2	DMC	676	Old Gold-LT
▢	~	2	DMC	677	Old Gold-VY LT
▢	-	2	DMC	754	Peach-LT
▢	L	2	DMC	932	Antique Blue-LT
▢	¬	2	DMC	948	Peach-VY LT
▢	n	2	DMC	3688	Mauve-MD
▢	>	2	DMC	3689	Mauve-LT
▢	/	2	DMC	3752	Antique Blue-VY LT
▢	0	2	DMC	3787	Brown Gray-DK
▢	<	2	DMC	3862	Mocha Beige-DK
▢	·	2	DMC	3865	Winter White

Floss Used for French Knots:

Symbol		Strands	Type	Number	Color
▢	●	1	DMC	3787	Brown Gray-DK

Floss Used for Back Stitches:

Symbol		Strands	Type	Number	Color
▢	▬	1	DMC	320	Pistachio Green-MD
▢	▬	1	DMC	553	Violet
▢	▬	1	DMC	554	Violet-LT
▢	▬	1	DMC	931	Antique Blue-MD
▢	▬	1	DMC	3787	Brown Gray-DK

Note:
Stitched on 28-count antique white Jobelan
(by Wichelt), over 2 threads

Passion

Nothing happens without passion. It is the fuel that fires hearts and minds to greater aspirations and achievements. After all, we might do things with a sense of drudgery and obligation, but those are never going to be things that make our hearts sing and help us truly show up in the world as who we really are! These two little designs have been devised to remind us of that fact on a daily basis. They would also make lovely small gifts for those around us who need gentle reinforcement when it comes to trusting their creativity and insight.

There is a Greek word, *meraki*, which basically means putting one's heart and soul into whatever one chooses to do—and to me that sums up the concept of passion perfectly!

Live Your Passion

This small sampler-style piece, stitched on a dark fabric with light threads and appliqued onto a felt cushion, has an antique/chalkboard look.

Fabric: 32-count cobblestone Belfast Linen by Zweigart
(stitched over 2 threads)
Stitch count: 73 wide × 51 high
Approximate size: 5 × 3¾ in. (12.7 × 9.5 cm)

Cut fabric to measure at least 8 × 6 inches (20.3 × 15.2 cm); fold in half and count out to start stitching at a suitable point. When stitching is complete, wash and lightly iron the piece, and then carefully trim the fabric around the stitching, leaving a margin of approximately ½ inch (1.3 cm). Cut two pieces of felt or wool in a color of your choice measuring 6 × 5 inches (15.2 × 12.7 cm). Carefully center and stitch the embroidered piece onto one of the pieces of felt using a running stitch.

Using a softly colored embroidery floss (2 threads), stitch the two pieces of felt together to form a cushion, using a blanket stitch and leaving a small opening at one side. Fill the pillow lightly with polyester fiberfill, and stitch the opening closed. Attach a small silver charm to the top corner of the pillow (optional).

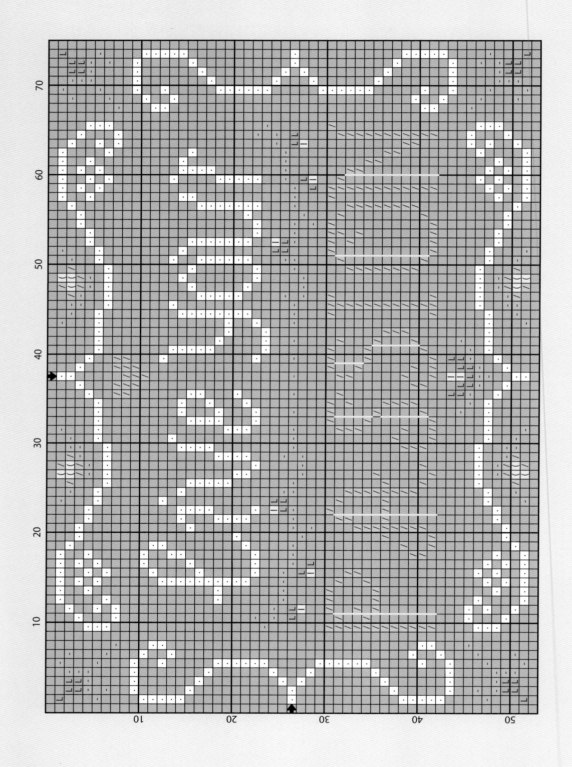

Floss Used for Full Stitches:

Symbol		Strands	Type	Number	Color
▨	/	2	DMC	754	Peach-LT
☐	[(	2	DMC	948	Peach-VY LT
▨	L	2	DMC	3042	Antique Violet-LT
▨	-	2	DMC	3813	Blue Green-LT
☐	I	2	DMC	3823	Yellow-UL Pale
☐	·	2	DMC	3865	Winter White

Floss Used for Back Stitches:

Symbol		Strands	Type	Number	Color
☐	∞∞∞∞∞	1	DMC	948	Peach-VY LT

Note:
Stitched on 32-count cobblestone Belfast Linen
(by Zweigart), over 2 threads

Do It with Heart

This second keepsake pillow is made in the same way as "Live Your Passion," but with different measurements, which are given below.

Fabric: 32-count cobblestone Belfast Linen by Zweigart (stitched over 2 threads)
Stitch count: 63 wide × 63 high
Approximate size: 4½ × 4½ in. (11.4 × 11.4 cm)

For this design, you will need two matching pieces of felt/wool measuring 5½ inches (14 cm) square. Follow the stitching and finishing instructions given for "Live Your Passion" on page 98.

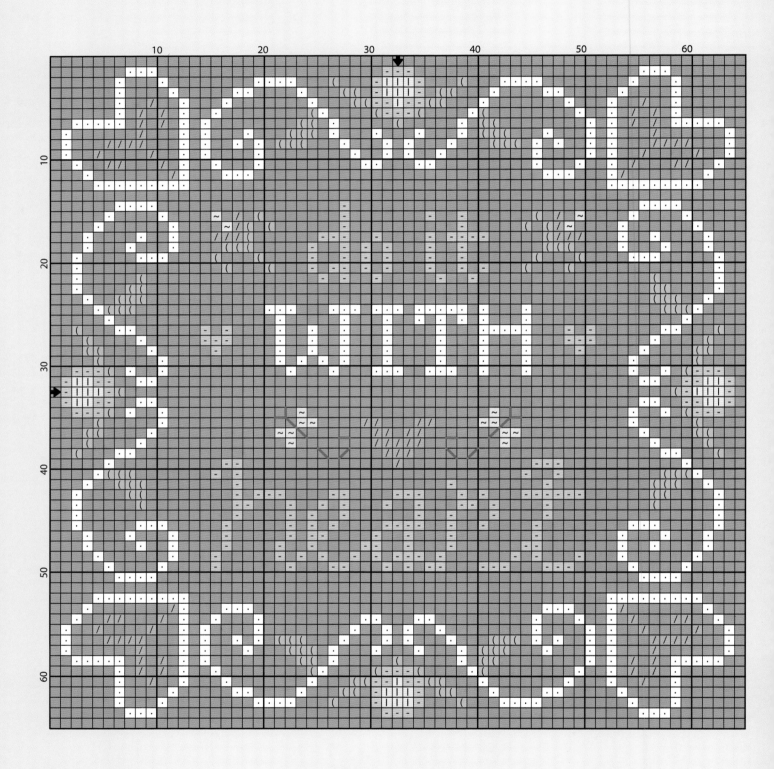

Floss Used for Full Stitches:

Symbol		Strands	Type	Number	Color
▨	-	2	DMC	754	Peach-LT
☐	│	2	DMC	948	Peach-VY LT
▨	/	2	DMC	3042	Antique Violet-LT
▨	(	2	DMC	3813	Blue Green-LT
☐	~	2	DMC	3823	Yellow-UL Pale
☐	·	2	DMC	3865	Winter White

Floss Used for Back Stitches:

Symbol		Strands	Type	Number	Color
▦	▬▬▬	1	DMC	3787	Brown Gray-DK

Note:
Stitched on 32-count cobblestone Belfast Linen
(by Zweigart), over 2 threads

3

CONNECT

It is in our connections with others and the world around us that we truly find our humanity and common purpose—whether these connections are with family, loved ones and friends, our pets, work colleagues, the wider community around us, and the beautiful natural life and living beings on our earth. There are so many everyday blessings to be found in life, and the awareness of this fact brings both joy and peace in the midst of what are often our hectic lives!

The designs in this section celebrate and honor these connections and blessings in various colorful ways and make great gifts or décor for the home. Stitch them with love in your heart and share them with those who make your life beautiful!

Love
Together
Heart's Blessing Gift Bag

Home
In Our House
Home

Nurture
Like Sunshine
Earth Angels

Life Is Sweet
Sweetie Pie!
Time for Tea

Celebrate
Happy Place
Celebrate Everything

Love

Love is the thread that binds our lives and our hearts to everyone around us—family, friends, loved ones near and far. Without love, there would be no context or true purpose to our being here on this earth. These two designs remind us of that in a simple and real way.

Together

There's an old African saying: "If you want to go fast, go alone. If you want to go far, go together." This is so true. When we are connected with others, we can tap into greater strength and purpose than we ever can on our own. Being together is truly the best place to be—as these two quirky and colorful birds remind us!

Fabric: 28-count China pearl Jobelan by Wichelt (stitched over 2 threads)
Stitch count: 70 high × 69 wide
Approximate finished size: 5 in. (12.7 cm) in diameter

Cut the fabric at least 8 inches (20.3 cm) square; fold in half and count out to start stitching at a convenient point. When the stitching is complete, wash and lightly iron the piece (if necessary). You will need a 6-inch (15.2-cm) wooden or plastic hoop to finish the piece: trim the fabric into a circle about 1 inch (2.5 cm) larger than the inner hoop, and then place the fabric over the hoop, ensuring that it is centered, and hold in place with the outer hoop, making sure everything is straight and secure.

Cover the back of the hoop with a circle of fabric. I use felt, which I then glue lightly in place. Lastly, add two ribbons, in complementary colors, for hanging the piece.

Floss Used for Full Stitches:

Symbol	Strands	Type	Number	Color
-	2	DMC	152	Shell Pink-MD LT
c	2	DMC	223	Shell Pink-LT
L	2	DMC	522	Fern Green
I	2	DMC	524	Fern Green-VY LT
n	2	DMC	644	Beige Gray-MD
~	2	DMC	778	Antique Mauve-VY LT
)	2	DMC	838	Beige Brown-VY DK
o	2	DMC	926	Gray Green-MD
/	2	DMC	927	Gray Green-LT
>	2	DMC	3364	Pine Green
^	2	DMC	3778	Terra Cotta-LT
<	2	DMC	3855	Autumn Gold-LT
v	2	DMC	3856	Mahogany-UL VY LT
(	2	DMC	3864	Mocha Beige-LT
·	2	DMC	3865	Winter White

Floss Used for Back Stitches:

Symbol	Strands	Type	Number	Color
———	1	DMC	838	Beige Brown-VY DK
———	1	DMC	926	Gray Green-MD

Note:
Stitched on 28-count China pearl Jobelan
(by Wichelt), over 2 threads

Heart's Blessing Gift Bag

Special people are truly a blessing to our hearts—and our lives. This little gift bag was created especially to remind those people of how important they are to us. The bag is a gift in itself, of course, but even more special when filled with a lovely present. It can also be used as a "blessing bag": a place to store special mementoes and memories, such as photos, dried flowers, and other things that remind us of the good and precious blessings we have in life!

Fabric: 32-count antique white Jobelan by Wichelt (stitched over 2 threads)
Stitch count: 79 wide × 79 high
Approximate finished size: 5½ in. (14 cm) square

Cut the fabric to measure at least 9 × 9 inches (22.9 × 22.9 cm). (You will also need a matching piece of fabric for the back of the bag.) Fold the fabric in half and count out to start stitching at a convenient point. When stitching is done, wash and lightly press the work (if necessary). Trim the fabric to measure 1½ inches (3.8 cm) all around the stitched area (this includes a ½-inch [1.3-cm] seam). Cut another piece of Jobelan to match this piece, and, with the right sides facing, stitch the two pieces together, but only down the sides and along the bottom—leave the top open. Turn right side out and press lightly.

Cut a piece of lining fabric of your choice (I used calico) to measure the same width as the bag but twice as long. Fold in the middle, and stitch down either side to make a square. Insert this lining into the embroidered bag, and fold down the top; stitch neatly in place all around the top of the bag. Cut two ribbons to the desired length, and attach them on either side of the bag, as shown in the picture (I added two mother-of-pearl buttons on top of the ribbons).

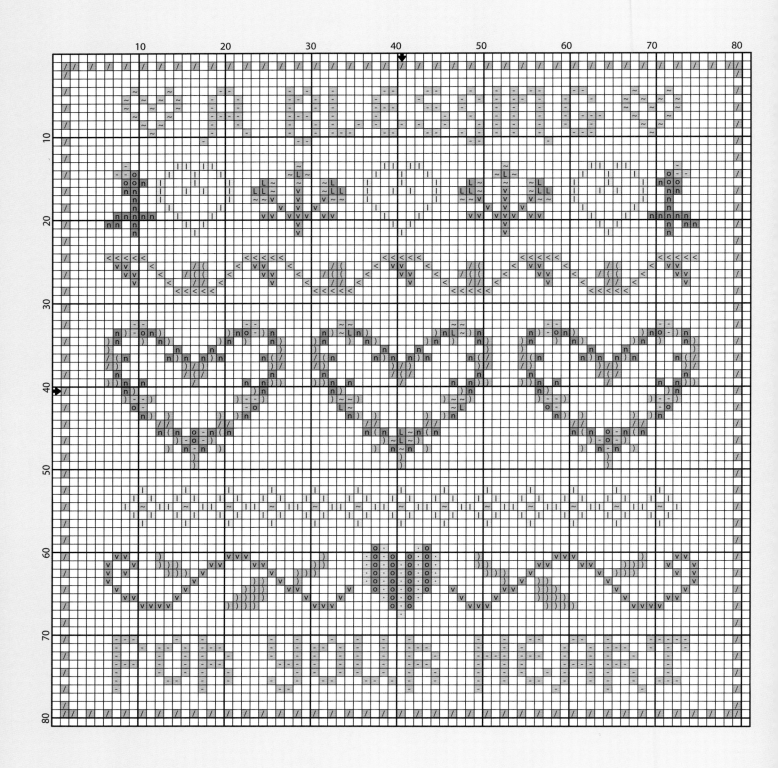

Floss Used for Full Stitches:

Symbol	Strands	Type	Number	Color
-	2	DMC	152	Shell Pink-MD LT
o	2	DMC	223	Shell Pink-LT
·	2	DMC	224	Shell Pink-VY LT
L	2	DMC	316	Antique Mauve-MD
n	2	DMC	522	Fern Green
)	2	DMC	524	Fern Green-VY LT
(	2	DMC	676	Old Gold-LT
l	2	DMC	822	Beige Gray-LT
<	2	DMC	3013	Khaki Green-LT
/	2	DMC	3042	Antique Violet-LT
v	2	DMC	3364	Pine Green
~	2	DMC	3727	Antique Mauve-LT

Note:
Stitched on 32-count antique white Jobelan
(by Wichelt), over 2 threads

our feet may leave

home

but not our heart

Home

Home is such a lovely and comforting word. There can't be many of us who are not moved or uplifted by thoughts and memories of our homes—past, present, or future. And, of course, home is not always just a physical place, built of bricks and mortar; it can be a feeling, a sense of comfort and joy we find anywhere—perhaps in a beautiful garden or sitting beside the ocean with friends.

In Our House

This design pretty much sums up what I feel makes a house a home (for me at least!). Love, hugs, and—always—cake and other good things to share! I created this piece on lambswool linen to give it a slightly antique and sampler look; it could also be stitched on dark gray/black fabric for a chalkboard style.

Fabric: 28-count lambswool Jobelan by Wichelt (stitched over 2 threads)
Stitch count: 45 wide × 115 high
Approximate finished size: 3¼ × 8 in. (8.3 × 20.3 cm)

Cut the fabric to measure at least 6 inches wide × 12 inches high (15.2 × 30.5 cm); fold in half and count out to start stitching at a convenient point. When the stitching is complete, wash and iron the stitching lightly (if necessary). This design is presented here as a simple hanging; the fabric was trimmed to around 1½ inches (3.8 cm) around the sides and base and 2 inches (5.1 cm) at the top. The top was folded over and pressed in place, and then a ribbon was inserted for hanging, held in place by 3 mini clothespins. (This design could also be framed.)

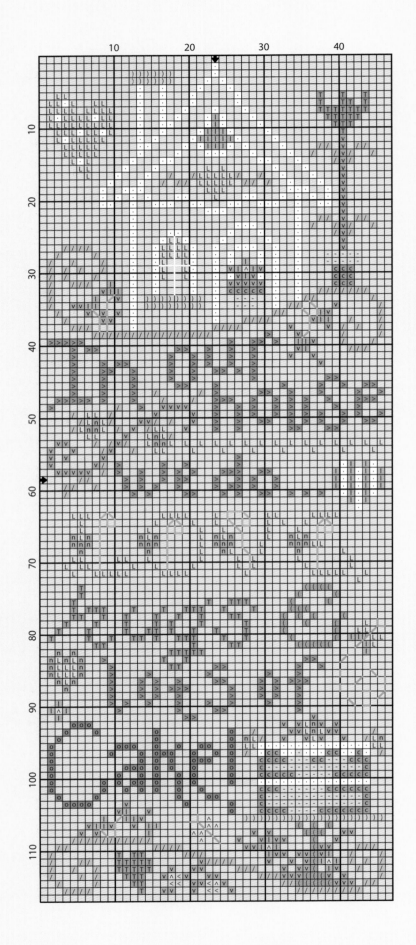

Floss Used for Full Stitches:

	Symbol	Strands	Type	Number	Color
	<	2	DMC	211	Lavender-LT
	n	2	DMC	223	Shell Pink-LT
	L	2	DMC	224	Shell Pink-VY LT
	T	2	DMC	316	Antique Mauve-MD
	>	2	DMC	926	Gray Green-MD
	(	2	DMC	927	Gray Green-LT
	)	2	DMC	928	Gray Green-VY LT
	o	2	DMC	3041	Antique Violet-MD
	I	2	DMC	3042	Antique Violet-LT
	/	2	DMC	3813	Blue Green-LT
	V	2	DMC	3817	Celadon Green-LT
	^	2	DMC	3855	Autumn Gold-LT
	c	2	DMC	3863	Mocha Beige-MD
	-	2	DMC	3864	Mocha Beige-LT
	·	2	DMC	3865	Winter White

Floss Used for Quarter Stitches:

	Symbol	Strands	Type	Number	Color
	I	2	DMC	3042	Antique Violet-LT

Floss Used for Back Stitches:

	Symbol	Strands	Type	Number	Color
		1	DMC	223	Shell Pink-LT
		1	DMC	3817	Celadon Green-LT
		1	DMC	3863	Mocha Beige-MD
		1	DMC	3865	Winter White

Note:
Stitched on 28-count lambswool Jobelan
(by Wichelt), over 2 threads

Home

A simple and so-very-true sentiment, presented as a simple, freestanding piece. (It could also be framed or made into a small pillow, if you prefer.) In addition, this design makes a great gift for people moving into their first, or a new, home.

Fabric: 32-count antique white Jobelan by Wichelt (stitched over 2 threads)
Stitch count: 87 wide × 49 high
Approximate finished size: 5½ × 3½ in. (14 × 8.9 cm)

Cut the fabric to measure at least 9 × 7 inches (22.9 × 17.8 cm); fold in half and count out to start stitching at a convenient point. When stitching is complete, wash and iron lightly (if necessary). Attach a small silver house charm or similar item, as indicated by the × symbol on the letter "O." You will need 2 pieces of light foam core board (or similar material); cut the first piece to measure 6½ × 4 ½ inches (16.5 × 11.4 cm), and glue a piece of thin batting or felt to one side. Stretch the stitched piece over this board, ensuring that it is centered, and then hold in place on the back of the board with double-sided tape. Glue a length of ribbon on the back of this piece, from one side to the other, as shown in the photo.

Cut another piece of foam core board to measure approximately 7½ inches wide by 5½ inches high (19.1 × 14 cm). Cover this piece of board with a suitable cotton fabric (or similar material), and fold the edges to the back, using glue or double-sided tape. Place the stitched piece centrally on the backing piece, and carefully glue in place; it's best to place it under a weight for a little while to ensure the two pieces are firmly affixed to each other.

our feet may leave

HOME

but not our hearts

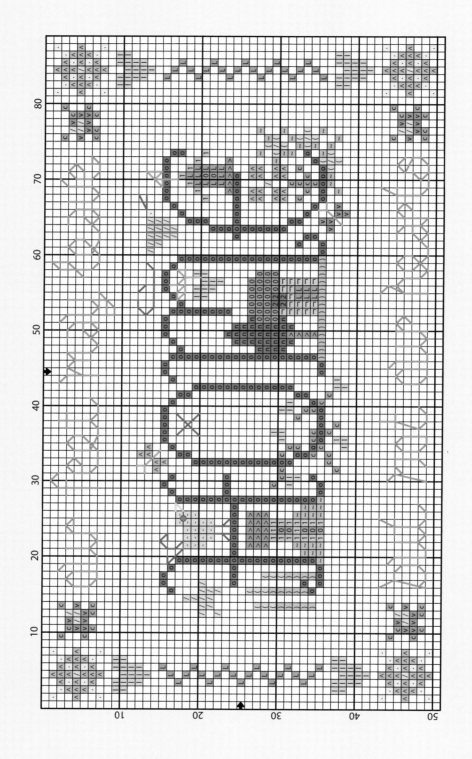

Floss Used for Full Stitches:

Symbol		Strands	Type	Number	Color
☐	(	2	DMC	153	Violet-VY LT
■	n	2	DMC	320	Pistachio Green-MD
☐	~	2	DMC	368	Pistachio Green-LT
☐	)	2	DMC	524	Fern Green-VY LT
☐	0	2	DMC	640	Beige Gray-VY DK
☐	¬	2	DMC	644	Beige Gray-MD
☐	1	2	DMC	738	Tan-VY LT
☐	^	2	DMC	760	Salmon
☐	I	2	DMC	761	Salmon-LT
■	o	2	DMC	931	Antique Blue-MD
☐	L	2	DMC	932	Antique Blue-LT
☐	c	2	DMC	3364	Pine Green
☐	·	2	DMC	3713	Salmon-VY LT
☐	2	2	DMC	3787	Brown Gray-DK
☐	v	2	DMC	3836	Grape-LT
☐	/	2	DMC	3855	Autumn Gold-LT
☐	>	2	DMC	3863	Mocha Beige-MD
☐	-	2	DMC	3864	Mocha Beige-LT

Floss Used for French Knots:

Symbol		Strands	Type	Number	Color
■	●	1	DMC	3787	Brown Gray-DK

Floss Used for Back Stitches:

Symbol		Strands	Type	Number	Color
☐	———	1	DMC	640	Beige Gray-VY DK
■	———	1	DMC	3712	Salmon-MD
■	———	1	DMC	3787	Brown Gray-DK
☐	———	1	DMC	3855	Autumn Gold-LT

Note:
Stitched on 32-count antique white Jobelan
(by Wichelt), over 2 threads

Nurture

One of the greatest gifts we have is friendship. It enriches our lives and makes us happier people on every level. So we should nurture our friends and all those who are dear to us, and also remember that even strangers are potential friends if we just reach out to them.

Like Sunshine

This piece shows one of my favorite sayings. I think it is so true. There are people who just make one feel better when they are around; they bring a warmth and grace even to difficult times and situations. These happy little bees buzzing around the sunflower remind us that we can find joy in other people—just as we can be like sunshine ourselves.

Fabric: 28-count star sapphire Jobelan by Wichelt (stitched over 2 threads)
Stitch count: 90 wide × 65 high
Approximate size: 6½ × 4½ in. (16.5 × 11.4 cm)

Cut the fabric to measure at least 9 × 6 inches (22.9 × 15.2 cm); fold in half and count out to start stitching at a suitable point. When stitching is complete, wash and press lightly (if necessary). You will need an oval premade canvas shape measuring 8½ × 6 inches (21.6 × 15.2 cm) and will also need to use it to cut a matching piece of light foam core board.

Glue a piece of thin felt or batting on the oval canvas, and then stretch the stitched piece over it, and glue or fix it in place on the back with tape. Cover the matching piece of foam core board with a suitable fabric, and glue in place on the back. Affix the two pieces together with glue, with the right sides facing out; place under a weight until the glue is dry. Glue a coordinating satin ribbon right around the oval to cover the join. Lastly, add a bow to the top of the piece, and hold in place with pearl-headed pins.

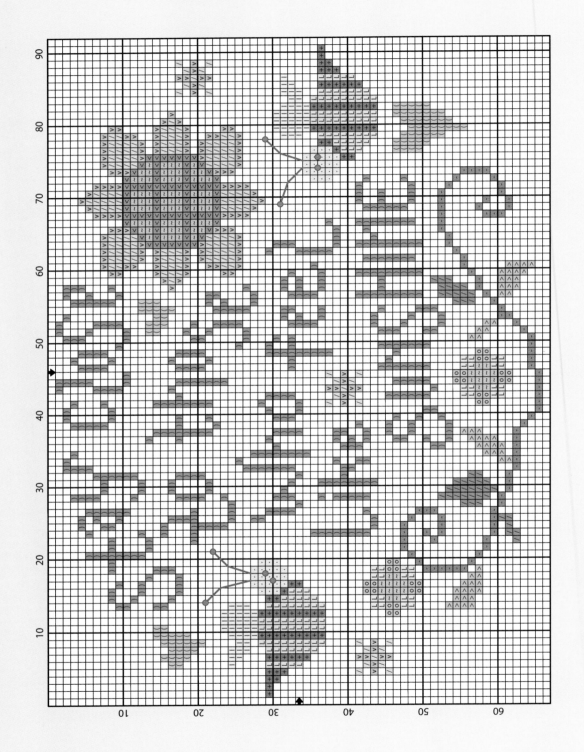

Floss Used for Full Stitches:

Symbol		Strands	Type	Number	Color
	~	2	DMC	738	Tan-VY LT
	L	2	DMC	744	Yellow-Pale
	((	2	DMC	754	Peach-LT
	o	2	DMC	758	Terra Cotta-VY LT
	·	2	DMC	950	Desert Sand-LT
	>	2	DMC	3013	Khaki Green-LT
	-	2	DMC	3052	Green Gray-MD
	I	2	DMC	3072	Beaver Gray-VY LT
	/	2	DMC	3363	Pine Green-MD
	))	2	DMC	3778	Terra Cotta-LT
	+	2	DMC	3787	Brown Gray-DK
	V	2	DMC	3854	Autumn Gold-MD
	/	2	DMC	3855	Autumn Gold-LT
	<	2	DMC	3863	Mocha Beige-MD

Floss Used for French Knots:

Symbol		Strands	Type	Number	Color
	●	1	DMC	3787	Brown Gray-DK

Floss Used for Back Stitches:

Symbol		Strands	Type	Number	Color
	——	1	DMC	3787	Brown Gray-DK

Note:
Stitched on 28-count star sapphire Jobelan
(by Wichelt), over 2 threads

Earth Angels

There are angels all around us, guiding, protecting, and caring for us every day. Some of them are unseen, and then there are the others who are very much a part of our lives— we call them our friends! Stitch this piece to celebrate a true friend, and personalize it with their name or initials to make it a truly lasting gift from the heart.

Fabric: 32-count antique white Belfast Linen by Zweigart (stitched over 2 threads)
Stitch count: 49 wide × 80 high
Approximate size: 3½ × 5¾ in. (8.9 × 14.6 cm)

Cut the fabric to measure at least 6 × 9 inches (15.2 × 22.9 cm); fold in half and count out to start stitching at a suitable point. When the stitching is completed, wash and press lightly (if necessary), and trim any loose threads of fabric. Cut a backing board of approximately 4½ × 6½ inches (11.4 × 16.5 cm) (I used foam core board), and then stretch the stitching firmly and evenly over the board, and hold it in place on the back with double-sided tape or glue.

(This design was personalized with initials. You can use any of the alphabets given in this book to do the same, or, alternatively, you could simply stitch another set of hearts/flowers in the space.)

Floss Used for Full Stitches:

	Symbol	Strands	Type	Number	Color
	/	2	DMC	152	Shell Pink-MD LT
	o	2	DMC	223	Shell Pink-LT
	<	2	DMC	522	Fern Green
	-	2	DMC	524	Fern Green-VY LT
	L	2	DMC	676	Old Gold-LT
	I	2	DMC	677	Old Gold-VY LT
	n	2	DMC	754	Peach-LT
	H	2	DMC	838	Beige Brown-VY DK
	1	2	DMC	932	Antique Blue-LT
	·	2	DMC	950	Desert Sand-LT
	((	2	DMC	3042	Antique Violet-LT
	))	2	DMC	3727	Antique Mauve-LT
	c	2	DMC	3863	Mocha Beige-MD
	~	2	DMC	3865	Winter White

Note:
Stitched on 32-count antique white Belfast
Linen (by Zweigart), over 2 threads

Life Is Sweet

This section is really just one for fun, to remind us how everyday pleasures like tea, cake, and chocolate are able to create a sense of joy and calm in the most hectic day! So stitch these pieces to remind yourself to slow down and enjoy the moment, either alone or with special people.

Sweetie Pie!

Stitched on soft pink fabric, this colorful little design makes me think of gingerbread houses and candy cane fairytales! For a different look, it has been finished as a small quilt-style hanging, with pretty pastel fabrics for the border. It could also be finished as a framed piece or even a small pillow.

Fabric: 28-count cherub pink Linen by Wichelt (stitched over 2 threads)
Stitch count: 63 wide × 63 high
Approximate size: 4½ × 4½ in. (11.4 × 11.4 cm)

Cut the linen to measure at least 9 × 9 inches (22.9 × 22.9 cm); fold in half and count out to start stitching at a suitable point. When stitching is complete, press lightly to remove any creases, and trim the design, leaving a border of 1½ inches (3.8 cm) all around the stitched area. (This includes a ½-inch [1.3-cm] seam allowance, which is also included in all the other fabric sizes given.)

You will need four different cotton patchwork fabrics in a suitable style and color (and a small extra piece of one of the fabrics for the hanging loops). Cut the fabrics as follows:

A: 3 × 7½ in. (7.6 × 19.1 cm)
B: 3 × 9¾ in. (7.6 × 24.8 cm)
C: 3 × 9½ in. (7.6 × 24.1 cm)
D: 3 × 11¾ in. (7.6 × 29.9 cm)

Stitch the fabric borders carefully onto the stitched piece, right sides facing and pressing seams open as you go; begin on the left-hand side with piece A, and then work clockwise around the design, ending with D at the bottom. Cut a piece of backing fabric (I used calico) to match the size of the finished mini quilt; then place the two pieces together, right sides in, and stitch together with a running stitch all around the quilt, leaving a small opening for turning. Turn the quilt right side out, stitch the opening together neatly, and press again. Cut two strips of patchwork fabric, measuring approximately 2½ × 7 inches (6.4 × 17.8 cm); fold in half lengthwise, and stitch along the length with a ½-inch (1.3-cm) seam. Press flat, fold in half, and attach to the top of the quilt on either side, as shown in the photo; stitch a suitable button onto each hanging, if desired.

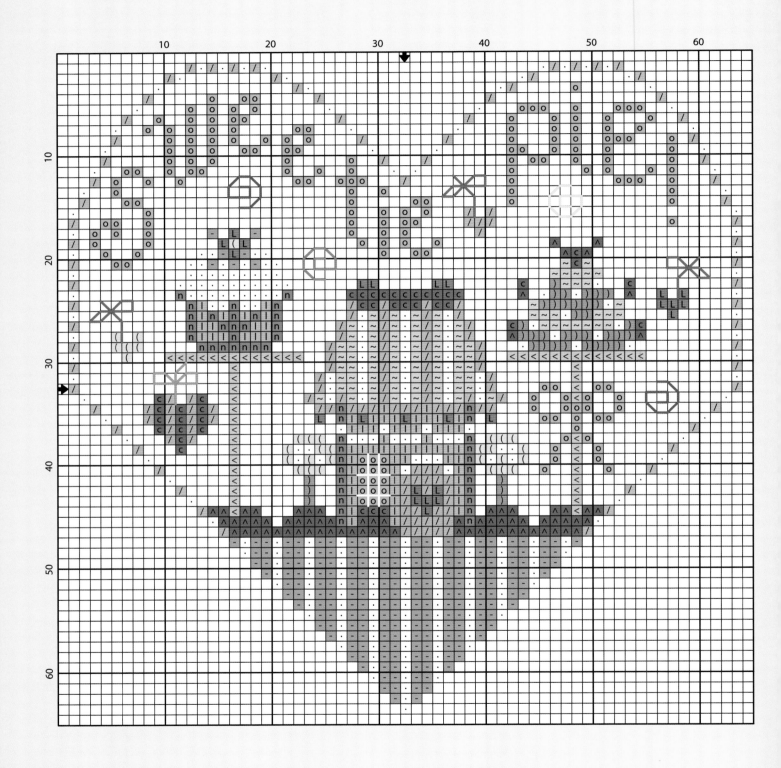

Floss Used for Full Stitches:

	Symbol	Strands	Type	Number	Color
	^	2	DMC	163	Celadon Green-MD
	/	2	DMC	210	Lavender-MD
	n	2	DMC	435	Brown-VY LT
	I	2	DMC	437	Tan-LT
	c	2	DMC	553	Violet
	<	2	DMC	644	Beige Gray-MD
	[(	2	DMC	744	Yellow-Pale
	o	2	DMC	760	Salmon
	~	2	DMC	761	Salmon-LT
	)	2	DMC	841	Beige Brown-LT
	L	2	DMC	3328	Salmon-DK
	-	2	DMC	3817	Celadon Green-LT
	·	2	DMC	3865	Winter White

Floss Used for Back Stitches:

	Symbol	Strands	Type	Number	Color
	———	1	DMC	163	Celadon Green-MD
	———	1	DMC	553	Violet
	———	1	DMC	744	Yellow-Pale
	———	1	DMC	841	Beige Brown-LT
	———	1	DMC	3328	Salmon-DK
	———	1	DMC	3865	Winter White

Note:
Stitched on 28-count cherub pink Linen
(by Wichelt), over 2 threads

Time for Tea

This pretty little hanging reminds us to take time for the simple pleasures of life, to relax and enjoy a few moments of mindful calm and peace. There is, after all, always time for tea!

Fabric: 28-count cream Jobelan by Wichelt (stitched over 2 threads)
Stitch count: 51 wide × 51 high
Approximate size: 3¾ × 3¾ in. (9.5 × 9.5 cm)

Cut fabric to measure at least 7 inches (17.8 cm) square; fold in half and count out to start stitching at a suitable point. When stitching is completed, wash and press lightly (if necessary), and trim the piece to measure 1½ inches (3.8 cm) around the stitched area. Cut a pretty, coordinating piece of floral cotton fabric to measure the same, and then place the two pieces together (right sides facing in) and stitch together, leaving a small opening in the bottom of the pillow. Turn to the right side and fill lightly with fiberfill or similar material, and then neatly stitch the opening closed. Attach a length of ribbon to the top left and right of the pillow, and hold in place with a suitable button. Tie the ribbons together for hanging.

Floss Used for Full Stitches:

Symbol		Strands	Type	Number	Color
	<	2	DMC	210	Lavender-MD
	-	2	DMC	211	Lavender-LT
	)	2	DMC	744	Yellow-Pale
	n	2	DMC	760	Salmon
	/	2	DMC	761	Salmon-LT
	(	2	DMC	822	Beige Gray-LT
	o	2	DMC	926	Gray Green-MD
	I	2	DMC	927	Gray Green-LT
	v	2	DMC	3363	Pine Green-MD
	L	2	DMC	3364	Pine Green
	·	2	DMC	3713	Salmon-VY LT

Floss Used for Back Stitches:

Symbol		Strands	Type	Number	Color
	———	1	DMC	926	Gray Green-MD
	———	1	DMC	3363	Pine Green-MD
	———	1	DMC	3790	Beige Gray-UL DK

Note:
Stitched on 28-count cream Jobelan
(by Wichelt), over 2 threads

Celebrate

Just being alive is truly a cause for celebration—even on difficult days, if we can remember that we will find renewed hope and strength. When you think about it, every day is pretty amazing, and it's in the simple things that we can often find the biggest blessings of all!

Happy Place

This is a colorful little pillow—very whimsical in style and quick and easy to stitch. Of course, our "happy place" isn't always a physical building. It can be a feeling, a memory, or time spent in a beautiful setting or with those we love.

- -

Fabric: 28-count antique white Jobelan by Wichelt (stitched over 2 threads)
Stitch count: 97 wide × 43 high
Approximate size: 7 × 3 in. (17.8 × 7.6 cm)

Cut the fabric at least 10 × 6 inches (25.4 × 15.2 cm); fold in half and count out to start stitching at a suitable point. When stitching is complete, wash and iron (if necessary). Trim around the stitching so the piece measures approximately 7½ × 3½ inches (19.1 × 8.9 cm). Cut a piece of light iron-on interfacing; iron it to the back of the stitching.

Cut two pieces of light wool felt, each measuring 9 × 5 inches (22.9 × 12.7 cm); center the design on one piece of felt, and stitch in place using a matching color thread. Then place the two pieces of felt together and stitch around them, using a blanket stitch and 2 strands of floss, leaving an opening in one side for filling. Lightly fill the pillow with fiberfill or similar material, and then blanket stitch the opening closed.

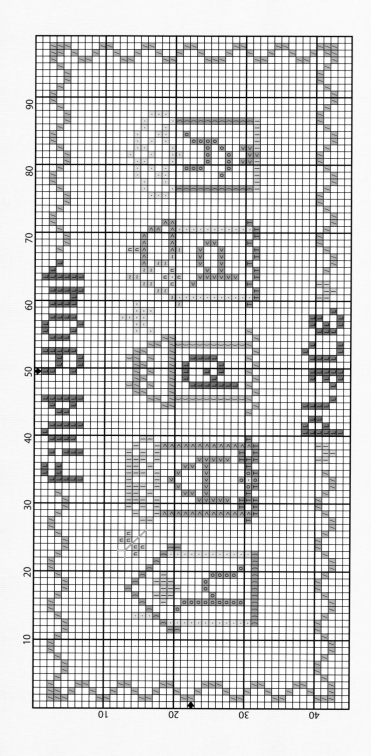

Floss Used for Full Stitches:

Symbol		Strands	Type	Number	Color
	n	2	DMC	153	Violet-VY LT
	T	2	DMC	503	Blue Green-MD
	<	2	DMC	554	Violet-LT
	>	2	DMC	642	Beige Gray-DK
	~	2	DMC	644	Beige Gray-MD
	(	2	DMC	738	Tan-VY LT
	)	2	DMC	3032	Mocha Brown-MD
	·	2	DMC	3033	Mocha Brown-VY LT
	o	2	DMC	3688	Mauve-MD
	I	2	DMC	3689	Mauve-LT
	/	2	DMC	3766	Peacock Blue-LT
	L	2	DMC	3810	Turquoise-DK
	-	2	DMC	3855	Autumn Gold-LT

Floss Used for Back Stitches:

Symbol		Strands	Type	Number	Color
	▬▬▬	1	DMC	642	Beige Gray-DK

Note:
Stitched on 28-count antique white Jobelan
(by Wichelt), over 2 threads

Celebrate Everything

This is a concept some people struggle with—for, to be honest, sometimes things happen in life that certainly don't seem to be any cause for celebration. I agree that loss, pain, and grief are not things we welcome on any level, but I have also discovered that when you look for the joy and peace in any situation (and there always is some!), the light comes through, even on what seems to be a very dark day. So I designed this simple and colorful "rainbow" piece to remind us to keep looking up and to keep looking for the good in every day.

Fabric: 28-count antique white Jobelan by Wichelt (stitched over 2 threads)

Stitch count: 55 wide × 55 high

Approximate size: 4 × 4 in. (10.2 × 10.2 cm)

Cut fabric at least 7 inches (17.8 cm) square; fold in half and count out to start stitching at a convenient point. When the stitching is done, wash and press the piece lightly (if necessary). Cut two pieces of light foam core board measuring 5 × 5 inches (12.7 × 12.7 cm). Cover one with felt and the other with a piece of suitable patchwork or cotton fabric, folding it to the back and gluing it in place. Stretch the finished embroidery over the felt-covered board, making it taut and centered, and then fold the excess fabric to the back of the board and hold in place with double-sided tape. Glue the two pieces of board together, right sides facing out, and allow the glue to dry. Finally, wrap a colorful ribbon around the sides of the boards to cover the join, and hold in place with glue. Add a loop of ribbon at the top of the piece for hanging.

Floss Used for Full Stitches:

Symbol		Strands	Type	Number	Color
▨	-	2	DMC	153	Violet-VY LT
▨	)	2	DMC	437	Tan-LT
▨	o	2	DMC	553	Violet
▨	L	2	DMC	554	Violet-LT
▢	(	2	DMC	744	Yellow-Pale
▢	/	2	DMC	745	Yellow-LT Pale
▨	c	2	DMC	760	Salmon
▨	I	2	DMC	761	Salmon-LT
▢	·	2	DMC	3713	Salmon-VY LT

Note:
Stitched on 28-count antique white Jobelan
(by Wichelt), over 2 threads

CHARTING AND CREATING YOUR OWN INSPIRED WORDS IN STITCHES

Adapting existing cross-stitch patterns or creating your own with words or sayings that are particularly meaningful to you is not difficult and is wonderfully rewarding. The designs in this book are such that many of them can be adapted in various ways, starting with the colors used. If you don't like the colors in a particular design, simply swap them out for ones that you prefer. (Just remember to keep the general depth of color in mind—darker shades and paler ones, as needed.)

If you wish to create your own sayings, it is possible to get several charting systems that make this process a breeze. I have used Patternmaker for Cross Stitch (a program by HobbyWare) for many years now and find it very easy and user friendly—but of course you may find another favorite.

Alternatively, most of my designs start life in the old-fashioned way, with a pencil, colored pens or markers, an eraser (very important!), and lots of graph paper. First, choose the count of the fabric you are going to use (28-count = 14 stitches to the inch; 32-count = 16 stitches to the inch). Work out how much space you are going to need for your chosen words/saying, and then measure this area out on the graph paper. Use a pencil to lightly sketch the words/quote in this space. Then fill in the blocks with lettering of your choice. You can use any of the ideas given in this book or the additional alphabet charts. Or you can make up your own lettering, as I generally do—there are no rules. Sometimes a word/saying is centered on the graph, and other times it is randomly placed down or across the piece, as you will see from the different designs in this book.

Do remember that writing in whole stitches is generally done in a paler shade of floss than backstitch lettering, which is done in a single strand of floss and so needs a darker or more intense color to stand out.

If you wish to change the words/quotes on any of the existing designs in this book, first photocopy the chart, enlarging it if necessary. Then cut a piece of squared/graph paper to cover the existing words, glue it down, and fill in the words of your choice.

Happy stitching and creating!

Floss Used for Full Stitches:

	Symbol	Strands	Type	Number	Color
■	o	2	DMC	931	Antique Blue-MD
■	-	2	DMC	932	Antique Blue-LT

Floss Used for French Knots:

	Symbol	Strands	Type	Number	Color
■	●	1	DMC	931	Antique Blue-MD

Floss Used for Back Stitches:

	Symbol	Strands	Type	Number	Color
■	——	1	DMC	931	Antique Blue-MD

Note:
Fabric varies according to the design being stitched.

VISUAL INDEX

Keep a Rainbow in Your Sky
6

Hope Is the Song of the Heart
10

Just Be You
16

I Am Enough
20

The Miracle in the Moment
26

Little Peace Garden Mandala
30

Beautiful Day

36

Let Go and Breathe

40

Choose Joy Today

46

Little Angel Mantra

50

Go with Your Heart

58

A New Journey

62

Dream Big

68

Make Your Dreams Real

72

Write from the Heart

78

The Beauty You Love

Bloom!

Lovely Day Angel

Live Your Passion

Do It with Heart

Together

Heart's Blessing Gift Bag

In Our House

Home

Like Sunshine
130

Earth Angels
134

Sweetie Pie!
140

Time for Tea
144

Happy Place
150

Celebrate Everything
154